God has a glorious plan for you! A big part of it is to love you into such a radical revelation of your God-given identity that you become utterly secure in who He created you to be. If that sounds like a great way to live, read Steve Prokopchak's book Identity: The Distinctiveness of You *immediately.*

– Robert Hotchkin, Men on the Frontlines Ministries

While reading this book, I had to put it down and process things repeatedly. It is incredibly convicting, causing me to face the insecurities and misguided loyalties in my life, but not once did I feel condemned or hopeless as I read.

– LaVerne Kreider, Co-founder of DOVE International

This book will help people in significant ways! The stories are so poignant and captivating.
– McClinton P.

Many will receive hope and transformation as they read this book. – Merle S.

What a great book to deal with all of the identity issues in our lives. Really appreciated how you shared on gender identity and sexual brokenness. I could feel the compassion. – Bonnie M.

Many of the issues you deal with in the book are instrumental to every one of us. Excellent job in making this a book for anyone at any age.
– John H.

These truths are so incredibly powerful!
– Josh G.

You did such a beautiful job bringing in God's perspective, especially on gender identity, and it was written so lovingly, clearly and with truth!
– Barb O.

It is taking me way longer than expected to work through your book. I am personally processing as I read and it is impacting me deeply!
– Nancy M.

My favorite and biggest revelation in the book is the story of the prison cell among the sheep in the field. That totally got me... Still processing that one.
– Rachel A.

IDENTITY
The Distinctiveness of You

Surrendering Who You Think You Should Be
to Discover Who You Are

STEVE PROKOPCHAK

House To House Publications
Lititz, Pennsylvania USA
www.h2hp.com

Identity: The Distinctiveness of You
by Steve Prokopchak

Copyright © 2021 DOVE International

Published by
House to House Publications
11 Toll Gate Road, Lititz, PA 17543 USA
Telephone: 800.848.5892
www.h2hp.com

ISBN: 978-1-7357388-3-3

Unless otherwise noted, all scripture quotations in this publication are taken from the Holy Bible, New International Version (NIV).
© 1973, 1978, 1984 by International Bible Society. Used by permission of Zondervan Publishing House. All rights reserved.

Contents

Thank you

Thanks to my wife, Mary, who never failed to say "yes" to read, re-read and edit as I wrote. You are my best, most favored critic.

Thanks to the many pre-readers who not only read this material to be sure it was user friendly, accurate and engaging, but also to those who took the time to respond to the many questions located at the end of each chapter. Your willing participation made a better book as you field tested this material.

Thank you to those who were so vulnerable to me by sharing their personal life stories of pain and victory.

Many thanks to Diane Omondi for her amazing ability to edit and give order to unclear sentences. Thank you to House to House Publications and to Sarah Sauder for her awesome design work with the book. I am grateful to each of you.

More so, I am indebted to the One who knew me before I was in my mother's womb—the One who called me into existence, healed me, and who has been doing a steady lifelong work of building His life within me. You are and will forever be my identity.

Introduction

Three clear sources were the motivation for this book. The first was a prayer tract that I had written many years ago for counselees titled *Who I Am in Christ*. The second was being approached by a pastor who stated rather emphatically that he needed a resource for his church body which expounded on that tract. He desired one which his church family could read and study in small groups to better understand and absorb the work of God's identity in his church families' lives. And the third was a survey I handed out to respondents in an attempt to discover where they found their security and identity.

That little prayer tract has sold by the tens of thousands. That pastor knew something about the need of his congregation to discover who they were, their security and their identity. And, from the survey, I astonishingly discovered that rarely was any respondent capable of ascertaining how security and identity come to us through our relationship with our heavenly Father.

These discoveries led to the writing of this book. Before writing, I voraciously read any related material that I could find (e.g., books, magazine articles, Google searches, scriptural searches and the like.) I immersed myself in attempting to discern who God says we are. I looked back over my own life, and I asked anyone and everyone who would give me some of their time to share anything they could concerning this subject. I have enjoyed every minute of it.

Collecting the personal stories for this book was fascinating. I was intrigued by the various testimonies of where each person was looking for identity and then how they actually found it in order to live a far more fulfilling life. While the names are changed, every word of their real-life stories is true.

My prayer for you, the reader, throughout this project has been two-fold. I long for you to discover the distinctiveness of who God created you to be and to personally sense His passionate love, acceptance, security, esteem and identity. Discovering those things provides no greater way to live one's life on this earth in preparation for the next life.

God has a destiny and a plan for every person He has lovingly created and longs to reveal that destiny. I pray this book helps you to personally discover that plan.

As you read, may you *be transformed from who you thought you were to become who God says you are*!

WAYS TO USE THIS BOOK

- **Personally study** and then answer the questions at the close of each chapter.

- **Use the book as a devotional** with its many scriptures and spiritual guidance.

- **Bring a small group together** and study chapter by chapter, receiving insights and stimulating group discussion toward personal healing.

- **The book is written for multiple generations.** Teenagers will be able to grasp and benefit from its truths. I suggest parents or teachers read the book with their teens and then discuss their findings together. Please pre-read chapters ten and eleven to be sure they are age appropriate for your children.

What marvelous love the Father has extended to us!
Just look at it–we're called children of God!
That's who we really are.
But that's also why the world doesn't recognize us
or take us seriously, because it has no idea
who he is or what he's up to.
But friends, that's exactly who we are:
children of God. And that's only the beginning.
Who knows how we'll end up!

I John 3:1, 2 The Message

I have eyes to see God's
eternal purpose.

II Corinthians 4:18

The Spirit Himself intercedes for me.

Romans 8:26

I am not condemned;
I have everlasting life.

John 5:24

I am saved and called,
not because of what I have done,
but because of the grace given to me
in Christ before the beginning of time.

II Timothy 1:9

The Idolatry of Insecurity and the Self-Factory

Most people are other people. Their thoughts are someone else's opinions, their lives a mimicry, their passions a quotation. — Oscar Wilde, *De Profundis*

Living for yourself is too notoriously small an aim for any human soul. — Klaus Bockmuehl

We would worry less about what others think of us if we realized how seldom they do. — Ethel Barrett

I have a friend, Sam. Sam is a truck driver by day, but a magician of sorts, a transformer of old cars, by night. Sam is a self-described "motorhead." Sam has the know-how, the expertise, and the skill to take an old car or truck in exceptionally rough or rusted condition and accurately turn it into a "new" one. He accomplishes what is known in his world as "frame-off restoration."

Sam tears apart every last piece, every single bolt and nut, and rebuilds the vehicle from the frame up. The process takes years, but when complete it is a piece of art, a work of beauty inspired and crafted with a distinct skill. Most evenings Sam has other motorheads using their specific skills working alongside him on the engine, the body, the electrical system, or the interior. These men share a commonality unlike most and a dedication to their craft that would rival any known club of the day.

For most of these men and quite often their spouses, these cars are their life. How so? Once completed, they wax and wax again and clean and shine because they will, on occasion, drive these beauties to a group meeting of motorheads called a car show. They will even win prizes for the best restorations.

These are not just cars; for some owners they become parts of their being, an appendage, so to speak. They find affirmation and attention through those cars. For others, it is almost as if they live their lives vicariously through their car. Their esteem, their security and even their identity can be wrapped up in that car.

Life without purpose?

I recently came across a greeting card that read, "This card has no purpose" on the front. Inside, the text continued: "I bought it anyway." I was a bit stunned at the greater truth of this card. Here's the thing with those words: how many of us suffer from the nagging thought of little to no purpose, but we exist anyway?

If I were to ask you to finish the following statement, how would you respond?

I develop a clear sense of personal security and identity from

_____

_____

_____

I have struggled with completing that statement, as would most persons. Quick and easy answers might not touch the core of identity. Answers that could be given include my job, my education, my house and things, my community position, my wealth, my family, my boyfriend, my spouse, or my ministry, to name just a few. We focus shortsightedly on stuff or earthly relationships that we think provide security, meaning in life and some form of identity.

Even though the above-mentioned answers are positive in nature, insecurity still wreaks havoc with many of us. The presence of insecurity in our lives fights with the human need of identity.

Defining your insecurity

What are some of your insecurities? What triggers insecure feelings in you? Write them down or make a mental list of them.

If you are having trouble making that list, let me help you with responses from a questionnaire taken several years ago. When asked what presented insecurity, honest responses included:

When I am anxious or worried
When I give in to fear
Not feeling as though I am good enough
Unsure if things will work out
Caring too much about what others think
Not feeling loved by others or by God
When I have needs that go unmet
Not feeling safe
Lacking confidence
A sense of helplessness
A deep sense of inadequacy
Being discovered that I am a fake
Not fitting in
An insatiable need for the approval of others
Inner turmoil from second-guessing my decisions
When I fail or quit a job that everyone loves me for

As you might have noticed, many of our insecurities are fear based. Most are connected to a life experience from our past. Based on those life experiences we are conditioned, perhaps without conscious awareness, to be fearful or anxious. We feel inadequate and our security level suffers. *Insecurities focus on what we feel we cannot do or on anxiety about what we might do in the future.*

You are not alone in your insecurities; we all have them. Comedian Ray Romano once said, "It's my insecurity that makes me want to be a comic, that makes me need the audience." Famous Hollywood actor Ben Affleck has been quoted as saying, "I'm always described as 'cocksure' or 'with a swagger,' but that bears no resemblance to who I feel like inside. I feel plagued by insecurity."

Let me share a secret with you. If you think about and talk about your insecurities, you are actually taking steps toward overcoming them and achieving a greater sense of security.

A scissors and my own insecurity

My father was a very harsh and demanding schoolteacher. He always seemed to know my teachers, even though he taught in a different school district. He demanded performance and excellence, although I can't remember one single time when he sat beside me and offered to help me with schoolwork or even read a book to me.

Report card time in my household was a tense time for me. I dreaded going home on those days. My grades were not that bad, but if I had a 'C,' he wondered why I didn't get a 'B.' If I had a 'B,' he thought it should have been an 'A.'

Once I even attempted to erase the grade on my report card, but it was quickly discovered that the grade had been changed. Even the most untrained eye could catch what I had attempted to do. But my fear was real because the consequences were real. I became nervous and more unsure of myself. This did not help my performance at all.

Several years ago, my mother brought with her a handful of my report cards when visiting our home. She had kept every report card from kindergarten on—every single one. Who does that? Wondering what I would do with them, I set them aside.

A few weeks later I began to peruse through them. My grades were quite good, especially in grade school and middle school. (High school might have been a different story with certain subjects… just saying.) However, it was a comment that my kindergarten teacher wrote on my report card that caught my eye. It read, "Steve has difficulty using a scissors." I failed scissors cutting! Really? Yes, really. (But honestly, could those dull, blunt-nosed scissors cut anything?)

Truthfully, I was nervous, even at that age. Apparently when taking a scissors into my four-year-old hand, I could not cut paper. It was an outer expression of an inner insecurity.

The short-sightedness of insecurity

A story in the Bible about a character named Hezekiah illustrates the selfishness of insecurity so well (II Kings 20). Hezekiah was ill and facing certain death. The prophet Isaiah went to him and said, "Put your house in order, because you are going to die; you will not recover." Hezekiah wept and prayed to God. And then God told Isaiah to tell Hezekiah that He would extend his life by fifteen years through the healing of his illness.

After this miracle, some visitors showed up from Babylon. Hezekiah made the mistake of showing off all his possessions and all the treasures of his forefathers. Isaiah questioned

Hezekiah about what he had done and then revealed, "The time will surely come when everything in your palace...will be carried off to Babylon. Nothing will be left, says the Lord" (Isaiah 39:6). Further, Isaiah revealed to Hezekiah that his descendants, his own flesh and blood, would be carried off to serve a foreign king in Babylon as well.

For most, this would be devastating news. But we might be surprised by Hezekiah's answer. "The word of the Lord you have spoken is good.... Will there not be peace and security in my lifetime?" (Isaiah 20:17, 18).

What short-sightedness on Hezekiah's part! He was only concerned about his own lifetime, his security, his well-being, and his peace of mind. Little did he care about the consequences of his actions for the next generations, even for his own family. Insecurity will do that. It is self-consuming. It is selfish and helps to create what I call the idolatry of self.

The idolatry of insecurity

In today's culture we are faced with an abundant supply of opportunities for self-worship. Look at how many decisions are being based on feelings rather than truth and facts. For example, to some people it is more important how they feel about a certain political candidate than what that candidate stands for. How we feel about math class and the teacher can override what grades we are receiving or how hard we are working.

The idol of self, a form of idolatry, causes us to be more preoccupied with our image, our own self-concerns, our need for affirmation, and the desire for attention from others. It is an excessive preoccupation with me, my feelings, my thoughts, and my opinions. In our book *Staying Together, Marriage: A Lifetime Affair* my wife and I wrote this concerning the idol of self: "When our identity becomes intertwined with our insecurity, we can become steeped in self-adoration."

In II Timothy we read a description of mankind in the last days. It is almost uncanny how accurately it describes what we can become when we worship ourselves and our needs only.

"But mark this: There will be terrible times in the last days. People will be lovers of themselves, lovers of money, boastful, proud, abusive, disobedient to their parents, ungrateful, unholy, without love, unforgiving, slanderous, without self-control, brutal, not lovers of the good, treacherous, rash, conceited, lovers of pleasure rather than lovers of God—having a form of godliness but denying its power. Have nothing to do with such people" (II Timothy 3:1-5).

These verses in II Timothy describe the idol of self extremely well. Though written many years ago, these words seem even more relevant today. Being "lovers of themselves" is not a godly trait, but an inordinate, self-focused, self-consumed factory of insecurity and lost identity. Like Hezekiah, in an attempt to find security, we become the center of our universe, yet sadly never discover who we really are created to be.

When I asked our questionnaire respondents where they thought their insecurities stemmed from, replies were:

Being raised in insecurity; volatile or unpredictable home

A major loss in life that you do not recover from

Never having been affirmed by my parents or other significant persons

Rejected by my peers

A negative, demeaning body image

Insufficient boundaries lacking guidance and discipline

Being overshadowed by an excelling sibling

The follow-up question to the above responses then became, "What are the personal beliefs that followed from this history?" It is surprising to note how many of these would be echoed by many of us. These are not unusual or one-off beliefs that stem from far-reaching and unusual life experiences, but rather, normal beliefs connected to our histories. See if you find yourself in any of the following responses.

I cannot accomplish tasks sufficiently.
I see myself as a failure.
I see myself as unattractive.
I see myself as a loser.
Not receiving affirmation or approval from others
I am a failure to others and to myself.
I do not fit in and I feel like a 'fifth wheel.'
I am incomplete in who I am.
Others do not respect me enough to listen to me.
I have nothing to give or to contribute.
I fear that no one will ever really love me.

Because of these beliefs as insecure persons, we struggle with our relationships. We walk out life with certain fears and ongoing feelings of failure. We struggle with our esteem and tend to retreat within ourselves. We become nervous around persons who we see as secure or from whom we sense an inner judgment. Some of us would claim that we are just shy, but the truth be told, we lack social confidence due to our own misbeliefs.

Going deeper, we can become emotionally dependent on others to provide us with security or find persons or substances that help to foster a false sense of security. It seems as if there is no end to our negative self-talk and repetition of neediness. How can something that each and every human being needs so deeply be so difficult to acquire? What makes security so elusive and why do we attach to it shallower forms of security?

The language of insecurity

Idolatry, or self-worship, will never build self-worth. Another amazing verse is found in II Kings 17:15. It reads, "They rejected his [God's] laws and the covenant he had made with their ancestors, and they despised all his warnings. They worshipped worthless idols and became worthless themselves. They followed the example of the nations around them, disobeying the Lord's command not to imitate them."

They worshipped God, but worshipped worthless idols as well. These were gods of their own making in accordance with their own cultural customs. This double-mindedness was passed on to the generations that followed. To this day, in this generation, we have persons who believe they are right with God even though they persist in going their own self-centered ways.

Did you notice that as they worshipped those *"worthless idols,"* they became *"worthless themselves?"* I do not claim to be a theologian, but worthless is worthless and worthlessness breeds more worthlessness. If worshipping self-created idols makes one worthless, no wonder we feel a sense of worthlessness while pursuing all kinds of non-worth-building desires and false securities.

We long for security, but gravitate to the stuff of earth—the things we can touch and see. Joyce Meyer said concerning insecure persons, "[They] derive their sense of worth and value from the acceptance of others rather than from who they are.... [They are] becoming approval addicts, always needing the approval of others to be happy and secure."

Attention from others will not build security

Actress Priscilla Shirer noted in an interview that some persons find significance in their career. When those temporal things are stripped away, they discover what their identity is actually based on. She admitted sometimes she tends to base her identity on "the opinions and acceptance of others."

Some of us use humor for attention. Some will use bizarre appearance, and others will starve themselves or gorge themselves, creating a pathway for food addictions. Still others will attempt to somehow make it rich, trusting that those riches will gain them the attention and notoriety they desire. Others will attempt to be perfect so that no one can find fault in them. This type of thinking results in perfectionism and keeps the perfectionist steeped in the idealistic, impossible goals of trying to always be the best.

The idol of self creates a vicious cycle of being self-consumed and self-absorbed. A whole factory of self-centered terms can be used to support this idol. Thousands of self-help books reinforce our self-centered behavior.

It is important to recognize that the gospel of self, driving us to seek comfort for the soul and purpose for life, will all too often end in self-hate, self-destructive behavior, loneliness, anger, and a slow death to one's emotional and spiritual being. The need to constantly project what others might be thinking about you or how they might respond to you causes mental fatigue. It is wearing to one's physical being. Exhaustion can set in, eventually leading to a "who cares anyway" attitude. Insecurity will allow the enemy of our souls to take us where we do not desire to go.

Proverbs rightly records, "The fear of man will prove to be a snare, but whoever trusts the Lord is kept safe" (Proverbs 29:25).

Insecurities can become identity attachments

Rushing to catch my next flight, I was walking vigorously through the familiar corridor of Terminal C at Chicago O'Hare International Airport. I caught a glimpse of a young man walking down the center of the two-way traffic wearing a tank top and rather short shorts with black high-top boots. He was completely covered in tattoos from the top of his head to his boot tops, including his neck and face. Numerous spikes were projecting out of the center of his hairless skull and more shiny things were protruding from his face and ears. It seemed everyone was trying not to look at him—yet could not stop staring at this unexpectedly different and strange-looking young man.

While I have no personal issue with tattoos, my heart immediately went out to him. Imagining he was comfortable with his look, so many were not. The attention he was receiving certainly did not seem positive. I began to wonder what provoked him to undergo such body image changes. I wondered what his story was and why he felt the need to do what he did to himself. Was he self-loathing or did he find comfort in the attention he received? His radical outward appearance seemed to be screaming a message from deep within his soul.

I would have loved to sit down beside him and hear his life story. I would ask him about his childhood. I would ask him about his life today, his job, and his thoughts about body image. I would inquire about where he finds security, identity, and purpose in life.

We each have a story. I find it intriguing when I have the opportunity to hear those stories, especially from strangers. Because I spend a lot of time on airplanes, I have occasion to listen to fellow passengers. I find most persons enjoy talking about their life experiences.

We could give many illustrations about where people find identity: art for the artists, music for the musician, successful surgery for the surgeon and so forth. I refer to these as identity attachments. They are careers or abilities that take on a life of their own and become one's identity.

Some identity attachments are positive, but some are very negative.

Negative identity attachments

Working with a drug addict for many years has given me a new appreciation of what persons with addictions suffer, not to mention what their loved ones suffer along with them. Drugs can take on a life of their own. A person can be a drug addict and work, earn a living, pay their bills, and participate in many activities. However, none of these will be their focus or define their purpose in life. They can have a family and even go to church, but those things will not capture their ultimate attention. What will? Drugs, and the need for more drugs.

A drug addict can eventually take on the identity of a drug addict because their lifestyle requires it. At the end of the day, all else takes a back seat to the most important thing in life—drugs. Please hear me, I am not saying for a minute that this life is chosen or preferred by these persons or that they are trying to be selfish. However, the addiction now leads them. It steals any worth, identity, security or self-esteem they might have and forfeits it all for the next "high."

In the book *Authentic Faith*, Gary Thomas quotes Gerald May when he speaks of the concept of the "addictive personality" and how harmful it may be. "May prefers to speak of an addicted personality. That is, the personality doesn't create the addiction; the addiction creates the personality."[1]

I have been lied to, stolen from, stood up, and have been the focus of bursts of anger because I am willing to confront the addiction in some of these persons. Addicts are often manipulative because they are trying to find a way around their relationships, not purposefully hurting those they love, but dodging them so as to avoid creating deeper pain. They also want to hide their own pain and addiction.

Other negative identities include strict religious upbringings or family cultures that perpetrate poverty or a poverty mindset. The actual religion could become less and less important while the religious culture takes over family identity and security.

Another huge identity attachment is long-term illness. I have heard people confess sickness to be "their cancer" or "my arthritis," as if it is their identity. It is not—and I believe the exposition in this book will explain why.

John of Kronstadt was a Russian Orthodox priest in the early 1800s. At that time in history, alcoholism was a major cultural problem. Most priests would not leave the parish. But John was compelled by his love for street people who were hungover and smelly. John would speak these life-giving and truth-filled words to a downtrodden person: "This is beneath your dignity. You were meant to house the fullness of God." And to the next needy one he would repeat, "This is beneath your dignity. You were meant to house the fullness of God."

People like John of Kronstadt see the value and the worth in humankind in greater measure than the pain-filled, hurting, addicted and insecure persons we are. Insecurity will provoke a never-ending striving for significance and identity, yet insecurity in and of itself provides no answers, only deeper feelings of inadequacy.

There is another voice

Can you hear the Father's voice saying, "This insecurity is beneath your true identity? This disease that has invaded your body is not who you are; it is not you. Your worship of yourself and your stuff ends in more pain; that is not my desire for you. I have a security that sets you free from all these things. I long to embrace you into eternity with me."

In the next chapter we will probe deeper into a level of insecurity that creates something called emotional dependency.

REFLECT AND DISCUSS

1. Did you create a list of your personal insecurities? If not, take time to do so now.

2. Can you discover where these insecurities originated? What were the precipitating life events that helped to create them?

3. How can these insecurities become self-made idols of worship? In other words, how have we made them life-consuming?

4. What language might we use to cover up our insecurities?

5. Can you pinpoint any identity attachments, positive or negative, in your life?

ENDNOTE

1. Gary L. Thomas, *Authentic Faith* (Grand Rapids, MI: Zondervan, 2002), 70.

I am now God's child.

I John 3:2

I am highly esteemed.

Daniel 9:23

I am held together by Him.

Colossians 1:17

Inwardly I am being renewed day by day.

II Corinthians 4:16

CHAPTER TWO

The Trap of Emotional Dependency

We know what we are, but not what we may be.
— William Shakespeare

[Security]: it's relationship over possession, intimacy over ambition, and service over selfishness. — Gary Thomas

My amazing mother was a hardworking hairstylist and worked most Saturdays. One Saturday, my Russian-speaking Ukrainian grandfather was in charge of my care until she returned home from the beauty shop. He loved mushrooms and mistakenly decided to pick some orange ones that were growing beside an old tree stump in our front yard.

You might be able to surmise these were no ordinary mushrooms, nor were they suited for human consumption. They were toadstools, a toxic and highly poisonous mushroom. My grandfather cooked them. They turned green and we ate them. My young body became ill, violently ill. When my mother returned home and identified what "Pop" had cooked for lunch, she gave me warm milk to expel the poisonous contents from my tender stomach. Then she rushed us both off to the doctor.

The doctor told my mother that she saved our lives by creating a way to rid the two of us of the toxins. My trust in my mother increased hugely that day and my dependency on her increased as well. I felt secure with her presence or just knowing she was in the background somewhere. From this and multiple other incidents in my life, she became a safe place to me.

The downside of having one's security in a human relationship is that one day that relationship will be gone, missing, or in some form unavailable. When we attach our security to a parent, a spouse, a girlfriend, or a significant other, we can essentially create more insecurity within ourselves. Looking to another human relationship for security—a security that can leave us or fail us—can be emotionally disastrous.

Emotional dependencies are counterfeits

When we solely look to another for our purpose, our meaning, our significance, and our security, we might find ourselves in an emotionally dependent relationship. Years ago, I wrote a book titled *Recognizing Emotional Dependency*.[1] One reason for writing the book was that few were talking about it and very little was written about the subject.

The story that follows is adapted from that book. While Elizabeth's name has been changed, the details are true and enlightening. Elizabeth created a lot of growth in us as leaders and in the members of our naïve and unsuspecting small group.

Elizabeth showed up at our small group study without warning one evening, followed by three squirming, unkempt and disruptive children. Soon this disgruntled woman had the whole group's attention. It seemed that life was impossible for her: bills were overdue, children were out of control, and marriage to a long-distance truck driver was so overwhelming that she seemed immobilized. Elizabeth was not shy about sharing her needs in our fellowship. She gravitated toward people who showed any interest in her life-controlling problems.

Many couples and individuals who tried to minister to her over time suffered burnout. No matter what they did, Elizabeth's emotional cup remained empty. Sucking the life out of small group members came naturally for her. "Seek first the kingdom of God" was not her "life verse." No one could ever seem to do enough to provide for Elizabeth's insatiable emotional needs. The more anyone attempted to do for her, the more she expected. Her needs for love, approval, and emotional "fixes" were voracious. Spending a whole day stationed in the kitchen of an unsuspecting small group member was not uncommon.

Why was Elizabeth's emotional cup so full of holes? I believe it was because her needs for security and significance were met only in imperfect human relationships rather than in a relationship with a perfect God. Elizabeth's emotional addiction was to people and the attention she could draw from them.

Foundations to emotional dependency

Everyone needs to know they are loved and approved of. Our first recognized source of love and approval is the family. Often, in dysfunctional homes, children may grow up with parents who are harsh, too strict, unable to be pleased, and critical. These parents control their children through shame and blame. The children can become guilt ridden, confused about authority, overly responsible, or compulsive. They frequently try to please their parents but seem to never quite measure up. In severe cases of this emotional roller coaster, self-identity problems emerge and a crisis of esteem ensues.

The second source of love, acceptance and approval is from God. I say "second" source because a child recognizes it after first having recognized a family's love and approval—or lack thereof.

Emma, a former counselee, was raised in a non-Christian home. Her father had wanted a boy and her mother had not wanted to be pregnant again. Emma tried all her life to please her parents. Her mother was often harsh and scolded her frequently. Emma sensed early in childhood that her sisters were treated quite differently by her parents than she was.

She worked hard in school for good grades and put every ounce of effort into excelling in sports. Although she was a bright student and an outstanding athlete, her accomplishments never seemed to earn those positive reinforcements of affirmation that she so desired from her parents.

Knowing that her dad had wanted a boy, Emma would spend most of her free time working with him on the farm attempting to do "boy's" work. She discovered that she was closer to her father than she was to her mother. Even so, that deep, nagging, gut-wrenching inner turmoil for unconditional acceptance and approval persisted throughout childhood.

Emma could not allow herself to relax. An inner voice constantly reminded her that she must always push forward to be busy and productive, since any benefit in life would come only by pleasing someone. With that deep longing for acceptance and love unmet, she told herself to just try harder again and again.

Elizabeth and Emma are both persons who are looking to other people to meet their basic needs of love and approval. These types of people continually find themselves in dependent relationships. Their thinking goes something like this: "If I can be good enough, do well enough, and not mess up, I am assured of so-and-so's acceptance and approval." The concluding thought is, "Then I'll be worth something."

Defining emotional dependency

The ingredients for an emotionally dependent lifestyle include insecurity (feeling helpless and hopeless), low esteem (not quite measuring up), dysfunctional family background (stunting emotional growth), being critical (of self and others), being fearful (fear of rejection, fear of confrontation), self-punishment (playing the martyr role), and a strong need for intimacy.

These needs and fears create a seedbed for one person becoming addicted to another person. In the booklet *Emotional Dependency*, Lori Thorkelson Rentzel defines emotional dependency as "the condition resulting when the ongoing presence and/or nurturing of another is believed necessary for personal security."[2]

We need others. I believe that relationship with God and with others is the most important thing in life. Jesus taught this principle when a Pharisee raised the question, "Teacher, which is the greatest commandment in the law?" Jesus replied that we were to "love the Lord our God with all our heart ... soul ... and mind ... and love our neighbor as we love ourselves" (Matthew 22:36-39).

Even within the importance of relationships, our need for relationship cannot be allowed to become the center of a person's life. The emotionally dependent person feels as though he or she cannot exist or function without a particular relationship. Mistakenly, this association is an attempt to meet the need for intimacy and security.

Signs of emotional dependency

The following are some signs Lori has included in her booklet as characteristics of emotional dependency. Reading through them should help you to identify emotional dependency in your life or in the lives of others.

- Either party in the relationship experiences frequent jealousy, possessiveness, and a desire for exclusivity, viewing other people as a threat to the relationship.

- Prefers to spend time alone with this friend and becomes frustrated when this does not happen.

- Becomes irrationally angry or depressed when this friend withdraws slightly.

- Loses interest in friendships other than this one.

- Experiences romantic or sexual feelings* leading to fantasy about this person.

(*Please note that "feeling" romantic or sexual toward someone of the same sex is not necessarily an indicator of same-sex attraction. This attraction begins in the emotional realm, and an unhealthy adult may begin to interpret this as a sexual attraction. At this point, the emotionally dependent person can choose to act out the relationship sexually, crossing boundaries they normally would not have considered crossing. This deepens the emotional dependency and promotes further confusion concerning sexual identity.)

- Becomes preoccupied with this person's appearance, personality, problems, and interests.

- Is unwilling to make short- or long-range plans that do not include the other person.

- Is unable to see the other's faults realistically.

- Is defensive about the relationship when asked about it.

- Displays physical affection beyond that which is appropriate for a friendship.

- Refers frequently to the other in conversation; feels free to "speak for" the other.

- Exhibits an intimacy and familiarity with this friend that causes others to feel uncomfortable or embarrassed in their presence.

Most dependent relationships are ingrown. Healthy relationships are open to others. The dependent person becomes jealous when others befriend his or her "special" friend. While healthy friendships can tolerate moodiness or a judgmental remark, the emotionally dependent person can be crushed by a certain look or comment from that particular friend.

Emotional dependency in the Bible

While the Bible does not speak about emotional dependence directly, we are admonished to be self-controlled throughout Scripture. Paul wrote in Titus 2:1-8 about sound doctrine.

"You must teach what is in accord with sound doctrine. Teach the older men to be temperate, worthy of respect, self-controlled, and sound in faith, in love and in endurance. Likewise, teach the older women to be reverent in the way they live, not to be slanderers or addicted to much wine, but to teach what is good. Then they can train the younger women to love their husbands and children, to be self-controlled and pure, to be busy at home, to be kind, and to be subject to their husbands, so that no one will malign the Word of God. Similarly, encourage the young men to be self-controlled. In everything set them an example by doing what is good. In your teaching show integrity, seriousness and soundness of speech that cannot be condemned, so that those who oppose you may be ashamed because they have nothing bad to say about us."

Older men and younger men, older women and younger women are all to influence one another with respect, self-control, faith, love, purity, integrity, and soundness of speech. If followed, these admonishments about relational self-control from Paul would help us avoid the emotional dependency trap.

Paul continues to apply this word in Titus 2:11, 12: "For the grace of God that brings salvation has appeared to all men. It teaches us to say 'no' to ungodliness and worldly passion, and to live self-controlled, upright and godly lives in this present age."

We can become vulnerable or susceptible to dependent relationships when we focus solely on our needs. When we lean too heavily upon one particular person, the emotional attachment can begin, causing us to lose objectivity in the relationship.

Jesus and His disciples

"What about Jesus?" we might ask. Did He have any form of dependency on His disciples?

Jesus was certainly intimate with His twelve disciples. However, Jesus had a strong sense of personal identity. He knew who He was. He knew that He had purpose beyond these twelve men. John records Jesus' prayer in John 17, capturing the thought that Jesus was aware of the extensiveness of His influence and authority. John 17:2 states, "For you granted him authority over all people that he might give eternal life to all those you have given him."

Jesus' prayer for His disciples is recorded later in the same chapter of John. In this prayer, Jesus was releasing the disciples to the care of His Father. He was not trying to control them or convince the Father that they needed to return with Him.

Take note of how Jesus maintained His focus on His Father: "All I have is yours, and all you have is mine."

At the same time, Jesus maintained an appropriate focus on His disciples:

"I pray for them. I am not praying for the world, but for those you have given me, for they are yours. While I was with them, I protected them and kept them safe by that name you gave me. None has been lost except the one doomed to destruction so that scripture would be fulfilled. I am coming to you now, but I say these things while I am still in the world, so that they may have the full measure of my joy within them. I have given them your word and the world has hated them, for they are not of the world any more than I am of the world. My prayer is not that you take them out of the world but that you protect them from the evil one. They are not of the world, even as I am not of it. Sanctify them by the truth; your word is truth. As you sent me into the world, I have sent them into the world" (John 17:9, 12-18).

Finally, Jesus also maintained an appropriate focus on followers:

"My prayer is not for them alone. I pray also for those who will believe in me through their message, that all of them may be one, Father, just as you are in me and I am in you. May they also be in us so that the world may believe that you have sent me. I have given them the glory that you gave me, that they may be as one as we are one: I in them and you in me. May they be brought to complete unity to let the world know that you sent me and have loved them even as you have loved me" (John 17:20-23).

In the above scriptures, it is clear that Jesus did not experience an unhealthy emotional attachment with His disciples. The language in this prayer conveys a healthy release of His closest followers to His heavenly Father.

Maintaining proper boundaries

Jesus knew His boundaries. By *boundary*, I mean *spiritual limit*. Jesus maintained appropriate limits or borders when dealing with people.

For example, how did Jesus approach the Pharisees? Did He stand back, wait, and watch to see if they approved of His works? No. When He did miracles or told them exactly who He was, they were right there to taunt Him. Jesus called them a generation of vipers (snakes) in Matthew 12:34. Again, in Matthew 15, He openly rebuked the Pharisees with comments like, "Why do you also transgress the commandment of God because of your tradition? ... Thus you have made the commandment of God of no effect by your tradition. Hypocrites! Well did Isaiah (one of their own) prophesy about you, saying: 'These people draw near to me with their mouth, and honor me with their lips, but their heart is far from me'" (Matthew 15:3, 6-8, NKJ). The Pharisees based their self-esteem and security in their outward appearance, but Jesus revealed that the inside of their cups was dirty.

To the woman at the well Jesus truthfully responded, "You are right when you say you have no husband. The fact is, you have had five husbands, and the man you now have is not your husband" (John 4:17, 18). Jesus did not become this woman's caretaker or rescuer. He let her know that He was fully aware of her lifestyle and current situation. In John 4:26, He revealed to her, "I who speak to you am he (the Messiah)."

Jesus knew this woman was trying to meet her inner emotional needs with men. Our Lord offered her living water that would flow like a river out of her heart—her innermost being.

Jesus knew that maintaining proper boundaries would maintain healthy relationships.

When unsure of identity, boundaries can be unclear

Christ knew that He was the Son of God. The disciples knew who had sent them out and who had given them the authority to do the works of God. In this way, they did not need to base their success on the approval or acceptance of others.

Emma, whom we discussed earlier, was unsure of her identity. Since it was a boy that her dad desired, she tried to do the things that she thought a boy would do. The goal to please her father cost her the development of her own identity. Emma's family patterns were the only patterns that she knew. A growing child does not possess the emotional or cognitive ability to recognize abnormal or dysfunctional family patterns. Consequently, some adults like Emma, when questioned about their childhood, would call their childhood normal when it was not at all normal.

Healthy emotions promote healthy relationships

If someone perceives that a specific relationship provides all his or her needs for intimacy, security, approval, acceptance, self-esteem, and friendship, it is understandable that the dependency will be difficult to break. Healthy emotions originate with a healthy relationship with God. He then gives us appropriate relationships with others.

Families can promote an unhealthy emotional dependency. When children do not grow beyond the healthy and normal dependency on parents or when parents desire to maintain an unhealthy dependent control over their children, the family can foster emotional dependency as well. Children who do not mature to become interdependent and eventually independent could become stunted or truncated for life. Further, it is a gross misuse of power when a parent chooses a child to be the adult in the family so the parent can be dependent on them. This creates an extremely unhealthy emotionally dependent relationship.

As parents, we create a healthy attachment to ourselves with our children for security and identity during a child's formative years. But if we continue that attachment into the teen years and beyond, the relationship can become unhealthy. As our children age through their teen years, healthy parents help them to detach so they can move toward independence.

For example, a father informs his 18-year-old son that he bought tickets for the basketball game Saturday night. The son informs his dad that he should have consulted him first; he already has plans with his girlfriend. After a noticeably quiet pause, the father responds, "Well, I guess I will just have to try to enjoy the game by myself. But it won't be the same without you. It's okay, son, go ahead with your plans." You can probably sense the unhealthy manipulation in this father's response to his son.

We should express love. That is a healthy emotion. We should be open to express both positive and negative feelings honestly. This is healthy as well. However, if we use our emotions to place guilt on another through manipulation, we have crossed a line.

This type of manipulation of emotions is destructive and unhealthy. When Paul wrote to the Thessalonians, he included a synopsis of how he related to them during his previous visit. Let's look at I Thessalonians 2:4-6.

On the contrary, we speak as men approved by God [They knew where their identity originated from.] *to be entrusted with the gospel. We are not trying to please men but God,* [They were not forming dependent relationships upon men.] *who tests our hearts.* [Allow God to "test your heart."] *You know we never used flattery, nor did we put on a mask to cover up greed—* [No emotional appeal through manipulation was found among them.] *God is our witness. We were not looking for praise from men, not from you or anyone else.*

These verses describe healthy emotions which, in turn, provoked healthy relationships absent of control and manipulation.

In the next chapter, we will look at the healing of insecurities. We will also go in-depth with building healthy identity in our children in chapter 16.

REFLECT AND DISCUSS

1. Have you discovered any relationships from which you derive a sense of security?

2. Have you experienced any form of emotional dependency that you were perhaps unaware of? How can you confront that area of your life?

3. How did Jesus maintain appropriate boundaries with His closest relationships when He was on earth?

4. What requirements or expectations do you put on close family or friends for your emotional well-being? What is the need behind these expectations? (For example, the need to be loved, valued, or the need for significance?)

5. How can you look to Jesus to meet that need? What truths from Scripture speak to that need?

ENDNOTES

1. Steve Prokopchak, *Recognizing Emotional Dependency* (Lititz, PA: House to House Publications, 1996).

2. Lori Thorkelson Rentzel, *Emotional Dependency* (Downers Grove, IL: InterVarsity Press, 1990).

I am justified from all things.

Acts 13:39

I am the righteousness of God.

II Corinthians 5:21

I am forgiven all my sins.

Ephesians 1:7

I will heal my people
and will let them enjoy abundant
peace and security.

Jeremiah 33:6

CHAPTER THREE

Healing Our Insecurity

*I will heal my people and will let them enjoy
abundant peace and security.* — God, Jeremiah 33:6

*Every insecurity I walk in has the potential
of becoming a security.* — The author

Many years ago, my wife and I were in a particularly difficult board meeting in which some false accusations were leveled at me as the leader of a ministry. The person speaking those words knew they were untrue. Others who were in the meeting also knew they were untrue. Yet everyone sat there allowing the false accusations to land squarely upon me. Perhaps in fear or perhaps in just wanting this meeting to be over with, no one except my wife came to my defense. Even she was quickly quieted.

I could feel that internal heat which physically arises when one is being shamed, embarrassed and scorned from a personal and dehumanizing attack. I found myself retreating inwardly, unable to resist the tensing of my neck muscles in particular, a place where I tend to carry tension. My emotions were running rampant. I hardly knew what feeling to feel or what thought to think. I was stunned at this totally unexpected, seemingly unfair, and obviously rehearsed imputation.

It was not pretty. The whole experience felt like a damning of my soul. The words stung me in my gut and I felt I had no recourse, no follow-up. I was silenced by the board and then the gavel descended with a resounding decision, a decision that would affect our immediate future.

After the meeting, my wife followed me to the parking lot for some fresh air. I was visibly shaken. "What just happened in there?" I asked. Dumbfounded, I then spoke out my honest thought, "How could he say those blatantly false things?"

Before she had an opportunity to respond through her tears, a car pulled up beside us. The driver, a board member who had said little in the meeting, rolled down his window. He looked directly at me without any hesitation and with a slightly bewildering, albeit incongruent smile, blurted out, "That was pretty hard-hitting in there. True or not, I would just say: after every death you die there is a promised resurrection."

He had some insight into death. He saw it in our faces. Perhaps he didn't intervene because this "death" was directed by the hand of God. Today I can say it was a profound, penetrating and enlightening moment for me. It was totally life-altering. Numerous insecurities, pride, and other areas in my life and my leadership began the painful, God-driven but mercy-led process of death.

Jesus said it this way: "If anyone would come after me, he must deny himself and take up his cross daily and follow me. For whoever wants to save his life will lose it, but whoever loses his life for me will save it" (Luke 9:23, 24).

In the book *Beyond Personality*, C.S. Lewis wrote: "Give up yourself, and you'll find your real self. Lose your life and you'll save it. Submit to death, death of your ambitions and favorite wishes every day and death of your whole body in the end; submit with every fiber of your being, and you will find eternal life. Keep nothing back. Nothing that you have not given away will ever really be yours. Nothing in you that has not died will ever be raised from the dead."[1]

Jesus' death

When the Savior died on the cross, He took the insecurities, pride, anger, sin and any other things we deal with to the cross with Him. There is absolutely nothing that He did not die for. He bore our insecurities, our false identities, our deepest issues and our most painful hurts. He died with them and for them on the cross.

Like a father who was also his son's judge in the courtroom, Jesus came down off the bench and paid the fine that God the Father had just levied on His Son. The judge, first a loving father, bore the penalty of the wrongdoing and paid the price of his son's fine himself. All the son had to do was receive the gift that his father, the judge, was freely and mercifully bestowing upon him.

Jesus' death is that gift given to us freely. His Father, our Father, sent His Son for the penalty of our sin when judgment should have come to us. There really are no earthly words for this. The best theologian, while being able to explain what He did, will never be able to explain why He did it except for one single word—love. Love motivated the Father and love motivated the Son. "For God so loved the world that he gave his one and only Son, that whoever believes in him shall not perish but have eternal life" (John 3:16).

Death leads to life

Here is a fact: Jesus did not stay dead. On the third day He arose and was resurrected to live forevermore. In the Gospel of John, Jesus said, "I am the resurrection and the life. He who believes in me will live, even though he dies" (John 11:25).

Because of this truth, the earlier truth comes alive as well: after every death there is a promised resurrection! This love story between God and man does not end at the cross. It comes alive with the resurrection of the Son of God, the first of many resurrections.

When a seed drops into the ground, receives water and sunlight, it will germinate. Though it were dead, it sprouts into new life. We witness this phenomenon regularly. How can something that was dead come back to life? Even though it happens every day in the natural world, it is still miraculous.

There is healing for insecurities and misplaced identities in this resurrection life. There is a new beginning—a fresh start. Though we were dead in our trespass, we will live again.

To die to ourselves as C.S. Lewis penned does not come easy. We fight it, wrestle with it, deny it, defend ourselves, project our shame and guilt onto others, and feverishly attempt to cover up our inadequacies. To die means to face all of these head on, acknowledge them, and confess them to God in order to eventually lay them at the cross.

Why do we hold onto something that inwardly is hurting us? We find it enormously difficult to be honest about ourselves. We can barely entertain the thought of looking into a mirror and saying, "You have deep insecurities and you have to stop covering them up." For some of us, letting go is more difficult because it demands a new way of living. It requires change. Sometimes change, even change for the good, is more problematic than staying the same, even when it is unhealthy to do so.

The two views of change

Some of us would resist moving the couch in the living room because we feel it is fine where it is. We might say, "It works for me. Why should I move it?"

I was recently conversing with someone about a huge change being forced upon him at his workplace. He told me,

"Everything is changing." I shared that sometimes change is simply inevitable. It is part of life, especially at our workplaces.

His reply? "It was fine the way it was for forty-five years. Things were working and now they are messing with what functioned so well… I hate change!" he declared.

Change is challenging, especially forced change. Why? When we feel forced to change, it means something we are presently engaged in needs to end or die. Almost any form of death is rarely easy or desired by us.

Other people, however, love and embrace change. My wife and I tend to be on differing ends of the spectrum when it comes to change. She is much slower at acclimating to change, sometimes resistant. I tend to like change. I want to move and live elsewhere; she wants to stay at the home we live in. I want to change cars; she is always satisfied with the one she's driving. We have adapted to this difference and, in fact, see it as a plus for our relationship. Just imagine if we were the same in one of these categories. We would either never change and be stuck, or we would constantly change and be in confusion or possible disarray.

When our children were young, we expected change from them, especially change from negative to positive behavior. Sometimes we helped to initiate that change by enforcing discipline. Why do we think that change should stop or that discipline for change should stop when we become adults?

Catch these verses in Proverbs: "He who listens to a life-giving rebuke will be at home among the wise. He who ignores discipline despises himself, but whoever heeds correction gains understanding" (Proverbs 15:31, 32).

The Bible tells us that God, like a loving parent, initiates discipline and correction. Do you know why? He loves us enough to encourage life changes. The Word explains, "God disciplines us for our good, that we may share in his holiness" (Hebrews 12:10). God wants us to change in order to grow and gain something good—to be like Him, holy. (See also Proverbs 12:1; 13:18; 15:32 and Revelation 3:19.)

What is security to you?

Before we move on, let's ask the question: what is security to you? Take a minute to write your answers. Below are some responses I received from my survey.

To be content
To have inner peace
Knowing I can be myself
To not be laughed at or made fun of
Not caring what others think
Having a stocked food pantry to be able to feed my family
Having my needs met
Being gainfully employed
Being with my family
Having a home to live in
Money in the bank
Solid retirement plans
Knowing I am loved by God
Knowing God is in control of my life

Have you been clinging onto insecurities that are now being identified? Have you attached yourself to false securities? Identifying these is so important to the process of healing. It is well noted that a doctor cannot prescribe a medicine or a treatment until there is a proper, exact and correct diagnosis. You just cannot take a chance on giving a patient the wrong medicine; it might harm them rather than heal them.

The same is true of all emotional healing. We need the Holy Spirit of God to place His finger on the exact area where healing is needed. I suggest you could stop reading and whisper a prayer in your own words asking the Holy Spirit to do this in your life. Be sure to write down what you hear.

If you are convinced that change is what you need and you are tired of making the same old insecurity-filtered mistakes, then let's get to some answers. It is possible to go from insecurity to security, but not based on our self-filled ambitions or human efforts.

Renouncing insecurity

It is imperative that we renounce the idol of worshipping oneself. To *renounce* means "to give up a claim" or "to disown voluntarily." Even if we are not able to pinpoint any specific self-protecting insecurities, we can still take a step of faith and renounce anything that looks like, smells like or acts like insecurity.

If we can label our insecurities, it is the right time to confess them. Perhaps as you have been reading this book, some of those insecurities have come to mind. It is now time to hand them over to God, renounce them, and break off any unhealthy dependency or unhealthy attachment with them. It is time to confess any fear of man that exceeds your fear of God. It is time to break off inordinate relationships that have become a source of security for you. It is time to lay down your excuses and justifications for negative behavior which stem from your insecurities.

"What agreement is there between the temple of God and idols? For we are the temple of the living God. As God has said: 'I will live with them and walk among them, and I will be their God, and they will be my people.' Therefore, 'Come out from them and be separate, says the Lord. Touch no unclean thing, and I will receive you.' And, 'I will be a Father to you, and you will be my sons and daughters, says the Lord Almighty'" (II Corinthians 6:16-18).

We must be fully convinced that our insecurities have created unhealthy dependencies within ourselves and with others. And then we must be fully convinced to give them up. No lasting justification can be found in insecurities. In giving them up to God we are saying we believe He holds the key to our security.

A closer look at justification

All of us have sinned. (Romans 3:23) We all fall short of God's plan, and the wages of "missing the mark" (which is the definition of sin) is death, but Romans 6:23 states: "The gift of God is eternal life in Christ Jesus our Lord." God has given us a free gift. Receiving it does not require any effort on our part.

There are three ways to define the concept of justification. (See Romans 5:1.) To be justified means that I am forgiven of my sin, I am free from my guilt, and I am in right standing with God. To be forgiven—set free of the guilt I feel due to my sin—and then to actually be in right standing with God in my human state is simply incredible. Words cannot express what has happened to me or how it has happened. Justification is a gift from God. Knowing that I am justified is the only true way to know peace in this life.

Can I be justified if I have committed sin? Yes, of course. There is no sin for which Jesus did not die. There is no sin that He has not already forgiven. Jesus forgave past, present and future sin over two thousand years ago. However, this does not mean that we can continue to sin without conse-quence. Paul addresses this: "What shall we say, then? Shall we go on sinning so that grace may increase? By no means! We died to sin; how can we live in it any longer?" (Romans 6:1, 2). Knowing we are forgiven by the Just One is never an excuse to continue sinning. God's grace has been freely offered to us through the sacrifice of His Son. We dare not take advantage of that grace just because we have been given a free will.

Our heavenly Father loves us so much that He does not force His way on us; we must choose His way. If we do not choose His way, we will suffer the consequences of our wrong choices. For example, if a man or woman engages in sexual activity outside of a committed marriage relationship, that person risks pregnancy or contracting a sexually transmitted disease. The consequences of their choices will exist even though their sin can be forgiven.

While justification is an act of God, we must choose not to allow sin to be our master. We are no longer under the law; we are under grace (Romans 6:14), but that is never an excuse to continue to do wrong and therefore crucify Christ again (Hebrews 6:6).

Severing unnecessary burdens

The burdens of perfectionism, bringing attention to ourselves, trying to live up to the expectations of others and longing for acceptance from those who we deem as important will need to be severed. When we endeavor to be all things to everyone without even knowing who we really are, a line of genuine identity and integrity has been crossed. We come to the realization that we are broken into pieces. We have given pieces of ourselves over to the control of others and have allowed them to dictate our identity to us.

At this point, we cannot even distinguish the real us. It is as if we are playing a character in a movie. That character is not our true self. Unfortunately, if we play that character long enough, we start to embrace it and become what we are not.

Jennifer came into our lives as a single mom, never married, although at the time she was living with her boyfriend. She not only lived with this man, but was raising her children in his house and driving his car. He paid many of her bills. All this created a connection that would eventually become this man's tool for controlling Jennifer's life. She knew she was not in right relationship with her heavenly Father, but she also knew that making a change would mean the loss of her home and loss of beds for her children.

My wife and I counseled her and prayed with her so that she would discern what she needed to do. We wanted her to make decisions on her own, becoming stronger in her faith in the process. Jennifer knew she did not possess the resources she needed for her family, but she was doing her best to learn that her heavenly Father did. We assured her she could trust Him if she would begin to sever those things that held her to a man who was not her husband.

Jennifer began to make difficult decisions. With each one, we watched God provide. First, a flexible job. Second, an apartment in an old farmhouse owned by a lovely couple that wanted to help her and her children. Then, our not-so-small small group took several offerings and bought her a car, breaking off the final connection to the man she once lived with.

God did it! With each huge wall Jennifer faced, she realized God had a plan for her to get over, around or through it. In this newfound relationship with her heavenly Father, things began to work out for the best for her and her children.

Putting our trust in God

We must stop trusting "self" and start trusting God. God's Word states clearly that He is our refuge, He is our stronghold, and He is our hiding place. "The Lord is a refuge for the oppressed, a stronghold in times of trouble. Those who know your name trust in you, for you, Lord, have never forsaken those who seek you" (Psalm 9:9).

Insecurities become a taskmaster that require us to trust ourselves. We have to find our way with those insecurities. If we desire to be free from them, we must do it on our own. But here's the honest truth: we cannot do it within ourselves. We rarely possess the personal strength and fortitude to change ourselves. How many New Year's resolutions have you made, only to fail to fulfill them a few days or weeks into the new year?

How does one trust God? Quite simply, we believe that He is trustworthy. I realize this sounds simple, but to some it is a giant leap of faith. And yet, we constantly jump into our car and trust that it will start. When we show up at work, we trust we are still employed. You have even trusted the chair you are sitting on right now to hold you and your weight. We trust the gasoline company to not fill the gas station tanks with water. We trust the grocery clerk to not overcharge us. We trust our credit card company to contact us when our card is illegally charged. Each and every day we blindly trust lifeless objects or other people. What keeps us from reaching out and saying, "Heavenly Father, I trust you"?

In order to fully trust God, we have to stop trusting ourselves or other human relationships. Life has taught some of us that most persons will eventually fail us. When that happens, we blame God and fall back to trusting ourselves. If you feel that God cannot be fully trusted, then you have effectively humanized God.

Perhaps you have felt let down by God. Perhaps there is a time when He did not come through as you had expected. Perhaps you are disappointed by a situation in which you feel He could have intervened. Whatever the reason, you now find it difficult to take that first step of trust.

When Moses asked God, "Who do I say you are to the people of Israel?" in Exodus 3, God said in reply to Moses that he was to tell them, "I Am Who I Am" (Exodus 3:14). God's description of Himself was "I Am."

I AM is the ultimate statement of self-sufficiency, self-existence and immediate presence. God's existence is not contingent upon anyone else. His plans are not contingent upon any circumstances. He promises that He will be what He will be; that is, He will be the eternally constant God. He stands, ever-present and unchangeable, completely sufficient in Himself to do what He wills to do and to accomplish what He wills to accomplish.

When God identified Himself as I AM WHO I AM, He stated that, no matter when or where, He is there. It is similar to the New Testament expression in Revelation 1:8, "'I am the Alpha and the Omega,' says the Lord God, 'who is, and who was, and who is to come, the Almighty.'"[2]

Frank Sinatra sang the song "I Did It My Way." Written by Paul Anka, it was a song about how the end is near. The lyrics are clear in that the songwriter was insisting on being able to do life his way. However, the truth is, we simply cannot do life by ourselves. Are you tired of doing life your way? In the long-term, it does not work—rather, it is exhausting.

In the next chapter we will further consider how to find more healing for our insecurities and the many ways they manifest in our daily lives.

REFLECT AND DISCUSS

1. How can you relate to the phrase, "After every death we die, there is a promised resurrection?"

2. In what ways does death lead to life?

3. Are you someone who embraces change or dislikes change? Why?

4. What are some areas that you have been clinging onto for security?

5. In what ways have you felt forced to trust yourself only?

6. In what ways do you identify with the phrase, "I did it my way"?

ENDNOTES

1. C.S. Lewis, *Beyond Personality: The Christian Idea of God* (London: The Centenary Press, 1945).

2. www.GotQuestions.org.

**You will be secure,
because there is hope.**

Job 11:18

I am chosen by Him.

II Thessalonians 3:5

God's love is lavished upon me.

I John 3:1

**God has given me a spirit of power,
of love and of self-discipline.**

II Timothy 1:7

CHAPTER FOUR

Have You Been Noticed Lately?

Stop defining yourself by yourself or others. Man has never had the power to change man. — Dan Mohler

Every other system says if you follow the rules...
if you perform, if you achieve then you're accepted.
Christianity says identity is NOT achieved; it's received.
— Timothy Keller

You have an ego—a consciousness of being an individual.
But that doesn't mean that you are to worship yourself,
to think constantly of yourself, and to live entirely for self.
— Billy Graham

One day while playing outside at our home, my five-year-old grandson said to me, "Papaw, did you see me make the basket?" He was playing with his child-sized basketball net. Those words—"did you see me?"—registered in my mind that day in a new way. They reflect our human craving for attention, approval and a "look at" from others.

My grandson longs for that voice of approval. After all, it's a child's thing, right?

Not so. Social media today has become an insatiable outlet for that same childlike desire. Facebook, Instagram and other sites are filled with pictures of our new hairstyles, our new recipes, our new homes, new songs, a new picture we painted, our child's report card of all 'A's or the new job promotion. It can be a "look at me; I need to be noticed" unending invitation. The troubling thing in our longing to be noticed, accepted and approved of is its complete focus on "me." Your Facebook fame might last a day or two. Your current "likes" might outnumber those on your last post—but then what?

We can unfortunately begin to define ourselves by the apparent impact we are making on social media. But these little approvals are temporal and short-lived. They do not have the power to build or rebuild our security.

We had a billboard in our town some years ago that read, "It's all about you, you, you!" Consumerism and commercialism have led us to seek first our needs, our rights, our self-care and our self-actualization. To deny ourselves anything is portrayed as failing to live the dream. When we become excessively self-involved and self-consumed, we no longer have time for others and can miss opportunities to touch lives around us.

Here is a truth: the more self-focused we are, the more insecure we will be. Being self-focused stunts our growth and essentially inhibits our security.

Comparison

One of the ways we focus on ourselves is through comparison. When my children were young, I wrote this story:

Maggie has never had a problem with her self-image. She loves life and makes the best of every minute. She loves people and believes that they all love and accept her unconditionally. Maggie has never stared into a mirror and felt hopeless. She's never even desired to look at herself in a mirror and make any kind of judgment. She is perfectly content with who she is, what she wears, the shape of her body, the color of her eyes, the size of her nose and the shape of her ears. Maggie blindly trusts in her Creator. She is content to be who she is. You see, Maggie is our yellow Labrador retriever.

The Bible tells us that comparison is unwise. "We do not dare to classify or compare ourselves with some who commend themselves. When they measure themselves by themselves and compare themselves with themselves, they are not wise" (II Corinthians 10:12). How so? When we compare ourselves to someone else, we typically come up short or proud. In other words, we either feel insignificant and inadequate, or we feel better than another—pridefully arrogant. Both of these outcomes are unproductive and self-deprecating, not to mention possibly hurtful to others.

Comparison does not build security in our lives. Paul the Apostle told Timothy, his spiritual son, to watch his life... closely (I Timothy 4:6). He did not tell Timothy to keep an eye on others, but rather to keep an eye on himself.

I Kings 19 indicates that when Elijah had eliminated all of Jezebel's false prophets of Baal, Jezebel sent a message to Elijah saying, "May the gods deal with me, be it ever so severely, if by this time tomorrow I do not make your life like that of one of them [the prophets of Baal]." He ran 'for dear life' into the desert. Elijah, soon after courageously obeying his God and proclaiming, "The Lord—he is God!" now decides to run with fear over one woman's fiery words of retribution. Even with Elijah's great feat behind him, he feels insignificant when comparing himself to the power of one woman.

"I" vs. "We"

Insecure persons excessively use the personal pronoun "I." They do not think in terms of "we" or "us." It has been said, "There is no 'I' in the word 'team.'" This is not the mantra of the insecure. They do not know how to freely give credit to others. Their need is to keep themselves front and center. They have to continually prove to others they are secure, of worth, and valuable. However, inside of this person, the feelings are just the opposite. Insecurity leads them to self-focus, keeping others informed of all their personal accomplishments through continuous self-accolades.

Leaders who struggle with insecurity find themselves internally competing with other leaders. They measure themselves by themselves, which Scripture states is unwise. That comparison normally leads them to either an inflated or a deflated ego. It will be difficult for such leaders to move toward any type of natural confidence because their confidence is often based on the fear of man.

The fear of man

Proverbs 29:25 states that the fear of man will prove to be a snare. What does that mean? The fear of man will trip you up. It will steal your direction, keep you from following God's voice, provoke stress and steal your joy. The fear of others' opinions of us is as old as time. It can be all-consuming.

Paul the Apostle was writing to the Galatian church about this very subject. In chapter one, he was saying how astonished he was that they would so quickly follow a false gospel and thereby desert the One who had called them. Paul then writes, "Am I now trying to win the approval of men, or of God? Or am I trying to please men?" (Galatians 1:10a)

Here is the question of questions for each of us to consider: who are we trying to please and whose approval are we endeavoring to win? Approval seekers will never be satisfied. Approval from others is an insatiable desire. If we are in need of the approval of certain others in our life, we will continually walk around with a soul and a spirit that is only half full. No relationship, no spouse, no job, no educational degree, no parent, no amount of money and no material thing will ever satisfy that life craving. *Who we think we should be based on comparison is actually less than who God created us to be.* The fear of man will only change you for the worse. When we change to become what we perceive others want us to be, we could inwardly be resisting the change, becoming angry, or shutting down our true selves.

Paul adds, "If I were still trying to please men, I would not be a servant of Christ" (Galatians 1:10b). Did he actually write that if we are continually trying to please men, we will not please Christ? What amazing insight Paul had into the heart of mankind. That scripture addresses insecurity and identity in a comprehensive way. It powerfully tells us that we need to make a deliberate decision to either serve God or serve man.

What are you embracing for your security?

Each of us needs to discover where our security is derived from. What things do we look to for security? The list can be quite lengthy.

Money	Success
Self-pride	Approval
Accomplishments	Business
Relationships	Marriage
Children	Houses and real estate
Retirement accounts	Reputation
Friendships	Material items/possessions
Titles and promotions	Assets
Art and crafts	Creating and designing
Position and roles	Heritage and family status

Employment	Education
Musical ability	Ministry
Past experience	School grades
Affirmation	Body building
Parents	Clothes
Appearance	Athleticism

What would you add to the list?

I am not saying that the above-mentioned sources might not provide some sense of security. For example, my wife prefers to travel internationally with me as her husband by her side. She feels safer and far more secure.

However, the reality is that any one of the listed items—or all of them—could disappear from our lives. Any number of them could be gone in seconds. In that case, what would we hold on to for our security?

Job lost it all

The book of Job in the Bible describes a life that was challenged—or shattered, really. Most of us, in Job's situation, would simply sink to the ground curled up in a fetal position. Job faced extreme loss. His security was severely tested. Job had seven sons and three daughters. He was a man of great wealth and resource. Scripture describes him as "the greatest man among all the people of the East" (Job 1:3). He was a God-fearing and righteous man.

First, Job experienced the loss of his livestock, his livelihood. Then he lost his farm workers and servants. Then the house where all his children were gathered collapsed on them and killed them. Following all this loss, Job became deathly sick with boils all over his body. What was Job's response to all this devastation? "Naked I came from my mother's womb, and naked I will depart. The Lord gave and the Lord has taken away; may the name of the Lord be praised" (Job 1:21).

Notably, Job's wife's response to all this disaster was interestingly different: "His wife said to him, 'Are you still holding on to your integrity? Curse God and die!'" (Job 2:9)

After such great loss, Job's wife leveled an accusation questioning why any man would hold on to his character and his integrity after such life-altering experiences. That might also be the view of the world around us. With security and significance found in our environment and our resources gone, why even uphold the value of life or desire to keep living? Job's wife was in essence saying, "Here is your chance, Job, to blame God, be profoundly depressed, wallow in self-pity, become mad at the world, question everything, and chant 'Why me?' to anyone who will listen." But this godly man did none of these.

Job's security was not in his wealth, his fame, his position, his family or his marriage. Job was a man who knew who he was outside of all his earthly possessions. This was a man who had a strong grip on the only One who could be his security, the only One who could redeem such a serious life cataclysm.

If you know the end of the story, you know that Job found prosperity once again. This time, it was twice as much as he had before this trial. Job 42:12 reports, "The Lord blessed the latter part of Job's life more than the first." Perhaps the biggest part of Job's test was not possessions or finances, but his heart. Was security rooted genuinely enough in Job's inner being that he could actually grow in his relationship with His heavenly Father rather than be forever angry at Him?

There is a pathway to security for every one of us. Like Job, I believe we are even more blessed when we find the right path, the path that God has already written for you and for me. We each need security in our lives, but how we go about seeking that security can be problematic.

The military

Can you recall a time when your security was rocked to the core? I mean devastation-level rocking? I can.

I had traveled all day, first on a bus, then on an airplane and once again on a bus, in order to arrive near midnight at Lackland Air Force Base, Texas. Fifty young men stumbled off the bus late at night with several drill sergeants already incessantly screaming at us. Not one of us knew how to stand at attention while we were being ordered to do so. The questions they were asking had never been asked of me before, at least not in the world I came from. Once in the barracks, the yelling, the cursing, the in-your-face high volume of verbal berating continued for several more hours. Finally, we were told to go to bed at 0200 hours, a bed that no one wanted to crawl into for fear of not being able to remake it in proper military style at 0500 hours, the announced wake-up time.

Lying in bed, I was longing for my mother and questioning what on earth I was about to encounter. I was a teenager, completely lost in a new world that was unrecognizable to me. My security sank to a new all-time low. In fact, if you had hooked me up to a security level meter, it would have read in the negative. I just can't adequately describe all the feelings one experiences within a few short hours of such trauma.

Missions

Just two years into marriage, my wife and I agreed to help start an outreach to adjudicated delinquent teenage boys. We would provide a home for up to six unruly youth, as well as emergency placements. We had a team of five staff persons. I was elected to be the leader because I was married "the longest." You can only imagine my hesitation.

I did not know what I was doing or how to do it. Leading within ministry was brand new to me. Besides, we were required to live by faith, with no guaranteed income.

It was a crash course on leadership, and it wasn't fun. My known world of security would be rocked once again. God was about to break me.

Have you ever felt as though you were in the wrong place at the wrong time? I felt that quite a few times, but it was because my insecurities were surfacing. Have you ever felt as though God dumped you on a deserted island to fend for yourself? I did, but it was connected to one thing: insecurity. Have you ever felt as though everyone you were trying to lead was against you or had a different opinion than you? I did, but like Job and so many others before me, God was in charge and determined to use all I was facing to grow me up. He was about to grab hold of my misplaced security and plainly straighten me out from the inside.

There were times I begged God to remove me from the insecure places in which I found myself, only to hear silence. I'll bet the three Hebrews Shadrach, Meshach and Abednego had some insecurity hesitations when they were being sent to Nebuchadnezzar's fiery furnace. But hear their expression, their faith-filled confession: "The God we serve is able to deliver us.... But even if he does not, we want you to know...we will not serve your [false] gods or worship the image of gold" (Daniel 3:17, 18).

How many times have you experienced the "but even if he does not" part of this confession? We desire to protect ourselves from the possibility of hurt or pain when perhaps our Father is calling us into a new life experience that will provoke immeasurable personal growth. I immaturely and prematurely wanted to be released from military boot camp, yet it did not happen. I had to determine, "but even if he does not," I will persevere and stick it out. When I felt that I did not have the faith or skills to lead as a missionary, I had to acknowledge that Christ in me is able and decide to stay on the task "even if he does not."

When all the wrong areas you have placed your security in are upended by the hand of God, you will need to decide who you serve, just like the Hebrew men did when faced with the fiery furnace.

Will the love and confidence you have found in a personal relationship with your Savior enable you to confront all the false sources of security in which you previously trusted? Will this confrontation lead you to abandon them in order to find the one and only security that will take you into eternity?

It's okay that you have trouble in this life. It's okay that you have been hurt. It's okay that you have suffered loss, because all of these are temporary. This life, this season, this walk, is temporary. Never is the trouble eternal and never is the hurt forever.

God so loved

God so loved you that He sent His Son, John 3:16 reveals. That verse does not say God was so frustrated with you or that God was so angry at you that He sent His Son. It says that He so *loved* you. Your inner dialogues about feelings of insecurity could be lacking this truth. It is a truth that will stop the endless search for security. When the love of God is present, fear, anger, unforgiveness, brokenness and insecurity begin to retreat. I may not be able to explain it fully, but I personally know it to be true in my life and the lives of many others. God's love fills every void.

If your focus is misplaced on someone's hurtful words or a personal attack against you, then you are letting that person and that voice determine your insecure, needy response. That inner voice and dialogue must include the voice of the Holy Spirit and the words of your heavenly Father. Left to our own thoughts, we can build a case against ourselves very quickly.

We are not just followers of Christ for our own personal health. We follow Him because He follows the voice of His Father and only speaks what the Father speaks to Him. (See John 5:19, 20.)

A secret to our personal healing is found in the life our Savior lived while on the earth. The Pharisees provided Jesus with many opportunities to walk in insecurity. They were constantly watching Him and waiting for Him to say or do something that they felt was against the law. Even when Jesus healed someone, if He did it on the Sabbath, they would persecute Him. But Jesus' secure reply was, "My Father is always at his work to this very day, and I, too, am working" (John 5:17).

Jesus walked securely, never riled by the false accusations of the religious ones of His day. He lived during the times of the Old Testament law yet at the same time was ushering in the New Covenant, a new kingdom government. How could He continually fight against the religious culture of His day? He was secure in who He was.

The security of Jesus

"For the Father loves the Son and shows him all he does. Yes, to your amazement he will show him even greater things than these.... He who does not honor the Son does not honor the Father, who sent him.... If I testify about myself, my testimony is not valid. There is another who testifies in my favor, and I know that his [the Father's] testimony about me is valid" (John 5:20, 23, 31, 32). What do you hear in your spirit from these verses? What challenges you and what connects or confronts you?

Regardless of how unfair or ridiculing or demanding the Pharisees were of Jesus, He never backed down from them, never acted insecurely, never questioned Who He was, and never questioned Who had sent Him or Who He represented. Later in the same chapter, Jesus honestly, forthrightly and with utter confidence in His heavenly Father said: "I do not accept praise from men, but I know you. I know that you do not have the love of God in your hearts. I have come in my Father's name, and you do not accept me" (John 5:42, 43).

God's love in our hearts

A secret found in Jesus' words above is, "I know that you do not have the love of God in your hearts." Jesus keenly put His finger on the insecurity found within the Pharisees and every other human soul. Without the love of God in our hearts, we are lost when it comes to finding a permanent source of security. There simply is none.

Knowing the love of God for us is our number one source of security and, as we find out later in the book, our identity as well. The Scriptures admonish us to "seek first the kingdom of God," (Matthew 6:33) but why would we do so if we do not know the love of the King of that kingdom? To not seek first God's kingdom is to actively seek first our own kingdom.

I spent many years as a marriage and family counselor. One day an ordained, denominational, seminary-degreed pastor came to see me. Several sessions into our counseling, he made an honest yet surprising confession. He said, "I am an ordained pastor who speaks on the love of God, knows the scriptures on the love of God and tells everyone that God loves them. But I do not know the love of God myself." Can you imagine that your profession is telling and teaching people that God loves them, and you yourself do not know that love?

It's an everyday occurrence. We think we know the love of God, but do we? Do we understand that deep within our twisted soul, our shortcomings, and our sins, God is madly in love with us? He created you because He loved you. He longs for you to know Him because He loves you. He forgave you through His Son's life given as a ransom on the cross because He loves you. He will receive you into eternity one day, not based on your accomplishments or anything you have done, but based on His incomprehensible, unfathomable, unexplainable righteous love.

Who really knows you?

Among all your relationships, who really knows you? Who knows your faults, your personal quirks, and your incapabilities? The Father, the Son, and the Holy Spirit really know you. Not only that, the Three-in-One, the Godhead, adores you. It is a revelation to know whose you are. It is a revelation to know the One who knows you inside and out. And, it is a revelation to know the love of God for yourself. Do you know this love? You can.

Please take time to read and to meditate on the scriptures below. Let the truth of God's Word sink into your spirit, your soul, your very being. The Bible records the words of Jesus when He said that the truth will set us free. (John 8:32) How? Because He is the Truth. Jesus also said, "I am the way, the truth and the life" (John 14:6). Any lies we have been believing would create just the opposite—bondage. Allow God's Word to loose you from the bondages of lies spoken over you or lies spoken by you.

I know I am loved and accepted because of the truth of these scriptures (abbreviated to help with memorization):

He is a faithful God, keeping his covenant of love to a thousand generations. Deuteronomy 7:9

I am loved with an everlasting love. Jeremiah 31:3

How priceless is your unfailing love, O God. Psalm 36:7

I trust in God's unfailing love for ever and ever. Psalm 52:8

I am a saint and loved by God. Romans 1:7

God's love has been poured out into our hearts through the Holy Spirit. Romans 5:5

I was loved by God before my birth. Jeremiah 1:5; Ephesians 1:4

Because of his great love for us, God, who is rich in mercy made us alive in Christ. Ephesians 2:4

And to know this love that surpasses knowledge, filled with the fullness of God. Ephesians 3:19

May the Lord direct your hearts into God's love. II Thessalonians 3:5

God's love is lavished upon me. I John 3:1

I am loved; God's Son sacrificed himself for me. I John 4:10

I am loved by Christ and freed from my sins. Revelation 1:5

And finally, these special verses:

For I am convinced that neither death nor life, neither the present nor the future, nor any powers, neither height nor depth, nor anything else in all creation, will be able to separate us from the love of God. Romans 8:38, 39

When you receive the unconditional love of the Father, who you are begins to drastically change. When we do not receive or know this true love, life is so much more of a struggle. What do I mean?

In resisting this love, we will struggle to let go of issues in our lives. We will struggle to forgive ourselves. We will struggle to forgive others. We will struggle to love and serve others. Without receiving this unconditional love, how do we possess the love and security to release those who hurt or wound us? How do we rise above our own insecurity enough to serve others?

In our insecurity, we want others to pay for their wrongdoing. But in the security given to us through the love of God, we long to share that love with others.

The following are seven deeper revelations of freedom tested in my life and the lives of others. They are practical, biblically guided steps that will result in certain freedom if applied by His Spirit to our souls.

Embracing seven revelations of freedom

1. **We cannot provide security for ourselves.** "For we are the temple of the living God. As God has said: 'I will live with them and walk among them, and I will be their God, and they will be my people'" (II Corinthians 6:16).

2. **God is our refuge, our high tower, our stronghold and our hiding place.** We cannot be that for ourselves. (Psalm 9:9; 31:4; 32:7)

3. **Our security is fully and totally in His acceptance and approval of us.** He has already accepted us and He approves of us. (Romans 15:7)

4. **The fear of man that leads to insecurity is replaced with the fear of God.** (Galatians 1:10) "They will have no fear of bad news; their hearts are steadfast, trusting in the Lord. **Their hearts are secure**, they will have no

fear; in the end they will look in triumph on their foes" (Psalm 112:7, 8, emphasis mine).

5. **We must cut off perfectionism, the attempt to bring attention to ourselves and the attempt to live up to the expectations of others.** We must release the weight of insecurity that holds us back and ties us down. (Acts 27:40 – cut loose the anchors of insecurity)

6. **Jesus broke off insecurity from us when He was on the cross.** He paid the price for our wholeness, our completeness and our security. Jesus took the curse of insecurity by becoming a curse for us. (Galatians 3:13)

7. **You were chosen in Him before creation.** You are not trying to win God's approval; you already have it. You are not an afterthought of God or a mistake. Your security comes from Him and Him alone. It is what He has already accomplished, not what you can do. (Ephesians 1:4)

Galatians 3:13

We will go back to number six above, the removal of insecurity through the cross of Jesus. Galatians 3:13 states so much for each of us and our personal freedom.

As you may be aware, the book of Galatians says quite a bit about the role of faith versus the Old Covenant law. It seems the Galatian church was being tempted to mix adherence to the law with obedience to the Spirit. Paul makes it clear that going back to observing the law would put them "under a curse" of the law. He explains that "no one is justified before God by the law, because 'The righteous live by faith'" (Galatians 3:11).

Paul, under the inspiration of the Holy Spirit, then writes in verse 13, "Christ redeemed us from the curse of the law by becoming a curse for us, for it is written: 'Cursed is everyone who is hung on a tree [a cross].'" What does this mean to you and me and our security? Jesus took each and every curse since the fall of man in Genesis chapter three upon the cross, spilled His blood, and died to defeat each and every one of them. He became a curse for us.

Astonishingly, that means Jesus took the curse of insecurity on the cross. He died for insecurity. He bore our insecurities upon the tree so that we would be free from every curse of insecurity. No matter the source of your insecurities, no matter your history with them or your family line of insecurities, they have all been nailed to the cross that Jesus our Savior died upon.

While the above truth is a reality of an act of God that took place over two thousand years ago, you must receive it for yourself and make it your reality today.

Now what?

Now we leave those insecurities on the cross. Now we accept and receive that the cross is between us and our insecurities. We are forgiven by the cross, cleansed by the cross, and given our freedom from any insecurity we have ever carried by the cross. They are not ours to maintain or hold onto; they are now released upon the cross of Calvary because Jesus died to take those insecurities upon Himself.

From the cross Jesus states, "You no longer need to carry one single insecurity. I died for them in order to set you free. Give them over to me." Further, because Christ did not stay on the cross or in the grave, we now have the power of the resurrection life to walk in continual victory over the curse of insecurity.

You can't do it anyway

God has seen you at your very worst and He is still madly in love with you. You are unconditionally loved by Him today and into eternity. There is nothing that you can add to what

Christ has already done on the cross to provide you with all the security you will ever need to live every day of life.

You can relax, take a deep breath, and receive what He has already provided for you. You can rest in His complete control of your life. Insecurity gives no peace. Isaiah 26:3 states, "You will keep in perfect peace him whose mind is steadfast, because he trusts in you."

You can bask in one more scripture from the book of Job as we close this chapter. "Life will be brighter than noonday, and darkness will become like morning. **You will be secure,** because there is hope; you will look about you and take your rest in safety. You will lie down, with no one to make you afraid, and many will court your favor" (Job 11:17-19, emphasis mine).

I know no greater place of security than the Father's arms. In His embrace He assures us of His love, acceptance and approval. In His arms He wipes away years of hopelessness and self-effort.

You are His and He is yours.

Consider joining me in this prayer:

Heavenly Father, just as You fully accept and love Your Son, Jesus, so You fully accept and love me as Your son/ daughter. That acceptance is not based on my history or anything that I have been able to do or accomplish. I recognize that Jesus paid the price in full for my sin and my insecurity. I am under no pressure to keep or earn Your love, acceptance, and approval because I already have it. I thank You that You replace my human efforts and attempts at being secure by Your death on the cross. Through Your shed blood, the curse of insecurity is completely broken off of me! I receive the security that only You can give to me through

Your Son. I am secure because Christ is secure within me! In His name I pray. Amen.

As we leave this discussion on security and begin to look more specifically at our identity, we will go back to Timothy Keller's quote at the beginning of this chapter. Concerning our search for identity, he said that every other world system tells us to achieve, to perform and to attain in order to be "someone," but Christianity teaches that our identity is not achieved, but rather received.

REFLECT AND DISCUSS

1. I wrote in this chapter that the more self-focused we are, the more insecure we will become. Do you agree or disagree with this observation? Why or why not?

2. How is comparison with others unwise?

3. Unlike Job, have you ever blamed God for severe loss in your life? Have you been able to work through those feelings?

4. How do you explain the concept of the love of God for yourself and others?

5. Return to the section in this chapter titled, "I know I am loved and accepted because of the truth of these scriptures" and meditate on each one of them. What is your heavenly Father personally speaking to you?

6. Review the "Embracing seven revelations of freedom" section. Be careful that you have thoroughly walked through each one. Take the time to look up each verse and allow it to speak to your spirit.

I can do all things through Christ.

Philippians 4:13

I am born of God and
I overcome the world.

I John 5:4

Christ's truth has set me free.

John 8:32

I am in Jesus Christ's hands.

John 10:28

I am God's house.

Hebrews 3:6

PART 2: IDENTITY

CHAPTER FIVE

The Loss of Our Identity and the Prison of Self

Think about what people are doing on Facebook today. They're...building an image and identity for themselves, which in a sense is their brand. — Mark Zuckerberg

Who has deceived thee as oft as thyself?
— Benjamin Franklin

There is plenty of security in a jail cell, but I have never heard of anybody beating down the doors to get in.
— William S. Broomfield

Our hometown newspaper carried an article recently about a local teen named Rowan. The article read, "Each day his alarm went off at 6 a.m. and he would roll over in his twin bed, grab his iPhone and start looking for memes—viral images and videos—to share on Instagram. He would keep searching and posting until it was time to board the bus for school. Between classes, at lunch and during study hall, he would keep his social media empire running with new images. His target was 100 posts a day."

Upon returning home for the day, "Rowan would turn on his laptop and sit in front of the glowing screen for hours.... His Instagram feed flashed before him like a slot machine." Rowan made decent money as well. Some months he made up to ten thousand dollars.

What was his goal? Was it fame? Was it money? In his own words, according to the article, Rowan said, "I want to have enough clout to be recognized for who I am.... I want to have connections everywhere and be financially secure." His business continued to grow as did his notoriety. Rowan was being noticed by college recruiters and being offered internships as well as jobs.

Then on July 26, 2019, Rowan's world turned upside down. His Instagram site was disabled—shut down without warning or reasoning.

Rowan's response? "A lot of my friends think I've become depressed, and I think that's right. I've been feeling insecure about a lot of things, like how I look and act and talk. I talk a lot less than I used to. I'm a lot less confident....I kind of just feel—I feel lost." Rowan's mother added that her son was not in a healthy state. His parents are trying to encourage him to engage with life offline.

Rowan's final comments about what happened to him and how he is now going to try another venue online is, "The more followers you have, the more voice you have... the more clout you have, the more power you have."

Without his online presence, Rowan's identity was challenged to his core. When that disappeared, he did not know who he was and struggled deeply. Rowan's voice, security, identity, relationships, "clout" and personal "power" were lost overnight. He now scrambled to find where he would fit and find that identity once again.

Where do I find my identity?

Henri Nouwen in his book *Who Are We?* shares five powerful lies of identity:

I am what I have.
I am what I do.
I am what other people say or think of me.
I am nothing more than my worst moment.
I am nothing less than my best moment.[1]

Is my identity found in my heritage or in my nationality or my ethnicity? Is it found in my political persuasion or my education? Can my identity be found in my sexuality or my gender? Is it found in my wealth, my work, my success, my abilities or my possessions? Can I find my identity in who I know or in the approval of significant others? Is it found in my appearance or my family name?

Is my identity found in my past losses or successes? If I have a sordid past, how is my identity played out in my present life? Have I used men or women to define me? Have I used poverty or wealth to define me? Have I used sickness to describe who I am? Have I given in to multiple lies about myself and completely lost any sense of who I really am?

Self-definition

Teenagers regularly seek out ways to define themselves. It seems to be part of the teenage lifestyle. Am I one of the smart ones, one of the athletic ones, one of the funny ones or one of the stylish ones, they might ask themselves. Identity can seemingly change annually depending on one's own self-perceptions and feedback from peers.

I read the story of a young lady who was on this search while in high school and finally landed her identity as being the "promiscuous girl." She said it was initially empowering. She could use this role to her advantage by getting anyone she wanted, for at least one night.

She shared that the Hollywood culture portrayed this sexual lifestyle as glamorous; everyone was doing it. In the end, she found herself in loneliness, emptiness and total despair, without any true or loving relationships.

Conformity vs. identity

Conforming to an identity due to our environment will not change our heart or who we really are.

For eight years, my wife and I ran a foster group home for court-appointed teenage boys. In those eight years, we had many different placements (young men and a few young women). Some of them truly changed and became successful, and some of them conformed. What do I mean?

If a foster child simply conformed to the requested set of rules, they were not changing. They may have succeeded in meeting their court mandate, but they would be back. How do I know that? Conforming to something does not change one's heart or one's identity.

If you are convicted of a crime and sentenced to jail time, you will conform to a life of incarceration and be labeled a convict. It is up to you whether you make changes while in this new environment. The environment may provoke change, but it cannot demand heart change. From this incarceration, you can conform to the image of a convict and learn new ways of crime, or you can refuse to be labeled a convict and change your heart to embrace a different identity.

This is why persons who lose weight, perhaps even one hundred pounds, can still see themselves as overweight. Even though their environment changed, their food intake changed, or their image in the mirror changed, their mind has not changed to receive the truth of a new identity.

Let's take this thought a step deeper.

The prison of self

During my counseling years, I practiced an example that helped counselees identify a prison into which they may have been inserting themselves. I called it *the prison of self*. While I cannot guarantee the thought to be original with me, here is what it looked like.

Imagine a beautiful, grassy field with a comfortably warm, bright sun shining overhead. There were sheep in this field— happy, unobservant, grazing sheep. The sheep did not have a single care in the world. Right in the middle of this beautiful field was a cold, dark, gray concrete constructed prison large enough for a single prisoner. There was a window with bars and a door with bars. Inside was a concrete slab for a bed with few further comforts of home.

It was inside this prison that you would find yourself counting the hours until the end of another day. All you did each and every day was to dream of being like those sheep who were grazing just outside your barred window without a worry in the world. It was a lonely place that caused you to feel like you were separated from the world. In that prison, you were left with only your quiet, self-generated thoughts.

But here is the interesting thing about this prison. The door is unlocked and open. You could leave anytime you desired to. The fact is, you are self-imprisoned. You can leave, but you choose not to. It is a prison of your own making. You can be like those sheep outside, but you remain inside. Why?

You stay in because "out there," you will need to see yourself differently. You will need to live free, act free, and be free. Choosing to stay in your prison of self is choosing to be dependent upon those who will bring you a meal, those who will tell you what you can do and what you cannot do. In that prison, you are not free, but you have come to depend upon those walls, those rules, and those limitations. In some weird way, you feel more secure within that confined space.

Counselee after counselee could see themselves within that prison through one life circumstance or another. It represented security to them. It represented a bit of necessary identity and clarity to who they were even if they were confined to that small space. They knew what would happen from day to day. It was predictable. It represented normality and came without surprises.

The man at the pool

The prison of self relates to a story found in the Bible in John 5. In the city of Jerusalem there was a pool called Bethesda. A great number of disabled people were there: the blind, the lame and the paralyzed. There was a man who was an invalid for thirty-eight years at the pool. Jesus approached him one day. Jesus, knowing his history, asked him an interesting question: "Do you want to get well?" Jesus did not assume anything. He knew this man was a long-term resident of this place and perhaps received daily care with a meal or two. It wasn't the greatest place, but it was a place to live, sleep, eat, have friends and hang out.

According to the Bible, this pool, at times, would be visited by an angel of God who would stir the water. When people were able to reach the water and get into the pool, they would be healed. The invalid's reply to Jesus was, "Sir, I have no one to help me into the pool when the water is stirred." But remember, Jesus asked him if he wanted to be well. Why would He ask a question with such an obvious answer? Hold on, perhaps there is an answer to this question that you have not thought about.

If Jesus heals this man and makes him well, the man will have to pick up his mat and walk out of that place. You say,

"That would be cool." Yes, but there is far more to this story than healing. That same man who was provided for because of his condition will now have to provide for himself. He will have to find a job, leave his friends, cook for himself and perhaps provide for his family. When Jesus asked the question "Do you want to be well?" He was really asking, "Do you want to leave this prison, provide for yourself by getting a job and leave what you have come to know as a long-term life?"

It's our choice

If I were God, I would give you no choice. You would have to leave. You would have to want to be well and provide for yourself. But Jesus was giving this man an opportunity to leave what he knew in order to live a totally different life with a totally different identity. For thirty-eight years this man lived one way. Now before him was the opportunity to live a very different life with an identity that was not connected to his illness or his environment. His hesitation or at least his excuse was, "While I am trying to get in, someone else goes down ahead of me."

Aren't we just like that man at the pool? We are not well yet we make excuses for ourselves to avoid change. "Trying" is not doing. Trying is saying, "I don't think I can do it, but I am going to tell you that I am *trying*." We imprison ourselves; all the while, the door is open. Change, living a different way, is scary to us even though being healed would be far better. Having to take full responsibility for where we are in life, what we believe and what we claim as our identity is just too frightening for some. It reeks of insecurity. We would rather stay where we are and complain about our condition, blame it on others or appease others by saying that we are "trying."

The more self-consumed we become, the more our identity is inhibited. Being self-consumed within a prison of self provokes a self-centered focus. We will never find an identity within ourselves of our own making. It will be false and will not provide a basis for living. It will be like the teenager who changes from year to year, trying to find where they fit in life and where they fit among their peers.

What was handed down to you?

I Peter 1:18 tells us, "For you know that it was not with perishable things such as silver or gold that you were redeemed from the empty way of life handed down to you from your forefathers." I am not here to blame anything on your parents or family line. What I desire to do is to cause you to think about what was "handed down" to you. What were some of those identity-forming beliefs handed down to you? What were those prisons that you readily accepted without question because they were all you knew?

I had a friend who was fearful of meeting new people. He would literally quiver, get his words mixed up and shy away from any setting where this might happen. One day we were talking about his history and he revealed to me that his mother lived in a constant state of fear of strangers.

One example he shared occurred while he was growing up on a rural Pennsylvania farm. His father worked away from the farm during the day. That left his mother and siblings home alone. Regularly, a traveling salesperson, grain or feed truck operator would show up. My friend's mother would lock the door and then hide herself with all the children in a small, dark closet. There they would stay quietly until the stranger would leave.

To this day, my friend is in a self-imposed prison when it comes to meeting new people. Each one represents something new to fear. It was a fear passed on to him by his "forefathers."

What are other causes of identity struggles?

What about a state of worry? When we worry, we are saying we cannot trust God, only ourselves. When we worry, we are expressing that we need to be in control; God is not. When we are consumed with worry or stress, we are saying that God is not big enough to handle our problems or the things happening in our life.

The loss of boundaries is another. Children need safe, secure, loving boundaries. When those boundaries are crossed or are nonexistent, children will feel insecure and will lack a sense of safety.

I read a story about a newly constructed school that had a new playground with no perimeter fence. During recess, the children hovered in the center of the playground near their teachers for security and safety. When a perimeter fence was installed, the children immediately went to the edges of the playground, feeling safe with the new fence—a new boundary. The fence gave them a sense of security and broader boundary lines. Were you trained as a child to worry or be in fear? It will affect your identity.

Sometimes a lack of trust is handed down from our forefathers. We are told to trust no one; not even God can be fully trusted. Families who believe this or unconsciously teach this to their children stay secluded in an attempt to protect themselves from having to trust others.

We are given a choice

It is important to ask ourselves a question: who determines or makes decisions for us? We should ask this about our past, present and even our future. What part does God have in those decisions?

If we allow life circumstances to direct us, or if we empower someone else to speak over us and determine who we are, then we are allowing someone or something else to determine our identity. We are given a choice to become what life hands us, or to be different.

Benjamin was born September 18, 1951, in Detroit, Michigan. Benjamin's father was twenty-eight and his mother was thirteen when they married. They lived in a 733-square-foot home. Benjamin was educated in Detroit public schools. When he was five years old, his parents divorced. His mother suffered severe psychiatric issues, attempted suicide and had several hospitalizations.

After the divorce and after discovering Benjamin was behind in his schooling, his mother required him to read two library books a week and complete a book report on each. When Benjamin finally graduated from high school, the *Detroit Free Press* ran an article that applauded him as receiving the highest SAT scores in twenty years of any student in Detroit public schools.

Ben wanted to apply to Harvard and Yale but only had enough money—ten dollars—for one college application. He was accepted by Yale and offered a full scholarship. Ben graduated from Yale and then graduated from the University of Michigan Medical School in 1973. He entered Johns Hopkins School of Medicine neurosurgery program. In 1987 Benjamin Carson was the lead neurosurgeon of a 70-member team who would perform a dramatic surgical separation procedure on conjoined twins. He was also the first neurosurgeon to perform successful surgical procedures on a child while still in the womb of the mother. He was the youngest chief of pediatric neurosurgery in the country at age thirty-three.

I am unaware of what was handed down to you by your forefathers, but I do have some idea of what our heavenly Father desires to hand you. It can be beyond your wildest dreams. Dr. Carson could have easily considered his past and told himself there was no future. His mother, his faith and his God told him otherwise.

Jesus expressed to us that we are to deny ourselves, pick up our cross and follow Him. What an opposite piece of advice from what we hear on a daily basis from our modern-day culture. How could one "deny themselves" and yet feel better about themselves? Jesus never once said that what we do for Him is who we are. In fact, He continually told the Pharisees of His day that this was not the case. It was not their outward appearance, their position in the local synagogue nor their memorization of the law that would determine their value or identity. In Matthew 23, Jesus spoke truth to the Pharisees and the Sadducees about finding their identity in all the wrong places.

We close this chapter with several deep-rooted questions. Meditate on and give honest consideration to these questions.

REFLECT AND DISCUSS

1. How valuable to God are you? In other words, how does God feel about you?

2. Who is God to you?

3. Who are you?

We will look at these questions closely in the next chapter.

ENDNOTE

1. Henri J. M. Nouwen, *Who Are We?* (Podcast audio course by Now You Know Media, 2017).

I was known by God before
I was formed in the womb.

Jeremiah 1:5; Ephesians 1:4

I am rescued from the
power of darkness.

Colossians 1:13

I am loved,
God's Son sacrificed Himself for me.

I John 4:10

I am born of the imperishable seed
of God's Word.

I Peter 1:23

CHAPTER SIX

Identity:
It's Not about You

*In the social jungle of human existence, there is no feeling
of being alive without a sense of identity.*
— Erik Erickson

Be yourself; everyone else is already taken.
— Oscar Wilde

H e was fifteen and his father brought him to me for counseling. Chris was multi-racial and the product of a rape.
He was adopted by a family who lived in Lancaster County,
Pennsylvania, two thousand miles away from where he was
conceived and born. He stated that he had no idea who he
was or why he existed. His face expressed confusion and he
was noticeably uncomfortable with the counseling office he
found himself in.

We had probably met for three sessions when I confessed
to myself that I did not know how to help this young man.
I did the thing that I always do when I come to that place:
I prayed. We stopped what we were talking about to pray
and ask God what He had to say to this precious young life.
In a minute or two I distinctively heard these words: "Tell
Chris that I (God) so much wanted him to be born. Tell him
that how he came into existence is far less important than
the fact that I called him into existence. I gave him birth; he
is My creation, My son."

That was it; that was the answer Chris was longing for. In one brief encounter with The Truth, The Counselor, Jesus, the answer to this young man's identity surfaced. His countenance changed, his eyes were brighter and a certain smile that said, "I now know" came across his face. It took the affirming words of his heavenly Father and the attention of the Spirit to call into existence a new man with a new purpose and direction for life. Chris came into the office that day filled with anxiety of the unknown, and he left with peace called forth by life-changing words of affirmation and identity. He had found new freedom for his very being and his personal journey ahead.

Three really important questions

We ended the last chapter with three questions. Did you find your answers to them? It was these same questions Chris was contemplating. How valuable to God am I (How does God feel about me)? Who is God to me? Who am I?

Every human being that ever lived or is now alive would like the answers to these questions. Chris's story illustrates the answers in a powerful way.

When we speak of value, we think of things that are valuable. Life is valuable! It is valuable to God. It is valuable because He has a destiny for you. It is valuable because He has purpose for you. It is valuable because He loves you just as you are.

He knew you before you were born

Just how valuable are you? God knew your value before your parents ever met. Your heavenly Father is so pro-life, pro-you, that He knew you before you were formed within your mother by the seed of your father. There are two important scriptures that establish this truth. It is radically essential that you capture this point in your spirit, not just your head.

The Old Testament prophet Jeremiah struggled with his identity and his self-esteem. He did not see himself as anyone or anything special. He was ordinary and young, just another human on the earth at his appointed time to live. In fact, Jeremiah once said to God, "Ah, Sovereign Lord…I do not know how to speak; I am only a child" (Jeremiah 1:6). God vehemently disagreed with Jeremiah and what follows is what God literally spoke over him.

"Before I formed you in the womb I knew you, before you were born I set you apart; I appointed you as a prophet to the nations" (Jeremiah 1:5).

It is enormously important to recognize God stating that before **He created you**, formed you in the womb (you are His creation), **He knew you** (He longed for you, had a plan and a purpose for you, desired you to live for Him, to know who you are in Him and to glorify Him in obedience all the days of your life). The sheer power of these words is almost incomprehensible for our finite, human minds to grasp.

We read something incredibly similar that Paul wrote to the church of Ephesus. It says, "For he chose us in him before the creation of the world to be holy and blameless in his sight" (Ephesians 1:4). **He chose you before the creation of the earth!**

Let's state these truths succinctly: 1. He created you. 2. He knew you. 3. He created and knew you before the foundation of the earth existed.

You are not a mistake. You are not a product of your environment. You are not lost in a sea of human beings, unknown to God. You are not less than anyone or anything. You are not judged by God. You do not anger God. In your mere existence, you absolutely thrill God.

Our first baby

Our firstborn was a son, Joshua Cale, weighing in at nine pounds and eight ounces. He was huge and he was perfect. We prayed for him even before he existed. We talked about him, dreamed of having a child, and longed to be pregnant. Once pregnant, we prayed over his development in his mother's womb for nine and one-half months. Arriving late, he finally came into this world screaming, making his presence known.

We loved him. We couldn't stop smiling around him. At his mother's breast, he began to bond with his parents. He recognized our voices from hearing us read stories to him and praying over him in utero. We called him Josh.

No one would separate us from him. No one would take him from us. No one loved him more than we did; we were his parents. There was nothing that he needed to do to earn our love; he had it in full. There was nothing that he had to accomplish to be part of our family. He was fully received, fully loved and fully accepted.

God stepped down from heaven and allowed humankind to enter into creation with Him. Together we created. Together we gave birth and together we would love without expectation. All Josh had to do was breathe, eat and make a mess in his tiny little diaper and we were fully thrilled with his mere existence. There was no earning our love; he had it from conception.

In this same way, you do not earn the right to be God's son or daughter. All you have to do is exist. He is simply delighted with you, thinks of you day and night and longs to be your parent and provide you with all the sense of identity you will ever need.

God affirmed His Son

Jesus' earthly ministry was about to begin. Most agree He was around age thirty. John the Baptist, Jesus' cousin, was preparing the way for Him. Jesus came to Galilee from Nazareth and there in the Jordan river was baptized by John. During this baptism, unlike any other, the Bible states the Spirit of God descended on Jesus like a dove. It was a visible presence of the Spirit of God. The only way the writer knew how to describe this occasion was that it resembled a friendly dove landing on a person's head.

This sign was then followed by actual audible words spoken from heaven. They were words of love, approval, affirmation, acceptance, security and identity. The heavenly Father of Jesus said, "You are my Son, whom I love; with you I am well pleased" (Mark 1:11).

Jesus' earthly ministry had not yet begun. He had not performed one single miracle at this point. Not one person had been set free from evil spirits and not one person had experienced a healing; yet God spoke such words of affirmation and love in His Son's mere existence. Not unlike myself as a parent, we loved our son before he could do anything, accomplish anything, communicate that he loved us, or earn his first 'A' on a report card. Our son was pleasing to us in his mere existence, as are you to your heavenly Father!

You are a miracle

Your life started as an egg. Human eggs are tiny, a single cell about the size of a period on a printed piece of paper—0.2 mm across. Your egg was formed in your mother when she was a tiny embryo. That makes you a lot older than your actual birth date.

For nine months a life is miraculously forming through the life of the mother in a watery world. Just the development of the human brain alone is said to be the most complex and orderly arrangement of matter in the universe. Our mind sets us apart from the animal kingdom by its ability to make moral judgments and discern between right and wrong.

You are some 206 bones anchored to muscles. Those bones can take up to 20,000 pounds of pressure per square inch, truly as strong as granite. Through this maze of muscle and bone run 60,000 miles of tubing that carry life-giving blood to every part of your body.

Putting all of these into action is a nervous system protected inside your spinal cord, channeling coordinates through a three-pound brain sending messages at 250 mph, faster than a Formula One race car. You truly are fearfully and wonderfully created. (See Psalm 139, especially verse 14.) Albert Einstein is quoted as saying, "There are two ways to live your life. One is as though nothing is a miracle and the other is as though everything is a miracle."

Your acceptance

You exist because God called you into existence. You are loved and accepted by Him because He loves and accepts you. All you have to do is breathe—and He is pleased with you. He says to you today, as He did to His Son over two thousand years ago, "You are my son/daughter, whom I love; with you I am well pleased."

Receive these words into your spirit right now, this very moment, because they are truth. Even if everyone else rejects you, God does not. He is pleased with you. You cannot earn His pleasure; you already have it. You cannot earn His love; you already have it. This is why you exist. This is how God sees you.

You are not who you think you are. You are who He says you are! If you are trying to be who you think others desire you to be, you will never be the person *He* desires you to be. It is said, "What you don't know won't hurt you." The truth is, what you do not know from God's truth and what you don't apply to your life, what you haven't heard and what you don't understand, could hurt you severely.

Psychologist and author Robert McGee said it this way: "Who you think you should be is less than who you already are." That is a statement worth reading multiple times.

To believe anything less than this is to be lied to. To receive those lies as truth will harm you forever. Stop living in anything less. Stop living in hurt, offense, disappointment or rejection. Start living through a revelation of His love, acceptance and approval of you. (See Romans 15:7.)

Freedom from our past

We will never find freedom attaching ourselves to rejections of the past, wounds found within our history or present disappointments. They are not who we are or who we are becoming. Never give in to the hurt from others, allowing them to be more powerful than God's truth. Never allow others to decide who you are. Jesus created you for His pleasure and only He knows who you really are. Only He can fulfill you, complete you and heal you.

The world of psychology teaches us that we are products of our past, our environments and/or our successes. Staying within this vein of thought, it means if we have nothing but horror in our history, we are less today than we were before those incidents. If we have been abused, molested, bullied, rejected or broken in some form or fashion, those painful experiences then define us. I believe God is here to say, to whisper in our ear, that our past losses, sins, mistakes, addictions or divorces do not define who we are today.

Mankind idolizes animals, nature, science, education, self-development, self-actualization and even unhealthy relationships over a personal faith and belief in a loving God. But His love through His cross transcends anything this world has to offer. Hear and receive Jesus' prayer for you in the following verses.

Father, I want those you have given to me with me where I am, and to see my glory, the glory you have given me because you loved me before the creation of the world. Righteous Father, though the world does not know you, I know you, and they know that you have sent me. I have made you known to them, and will continue to make you known in order that the love you have for me may be in them and that I myself may be in them (John 17:24-26).

Can you accept Jesus' prayer for you? Can you hear Him receive His Father's love before the creation of the world just like He asks you to? Do you know in your heart that God sent His Son for you? Have you confessed Him as Lord of your life, asked His forgiveness of your sins and entered a personal relationship with Him? Is His love in you as He prayed for it to be? Finally, did you catch that Jesus Christ, the Son of God, resides in you after you accept Him? There is no greater expression of love, acceptance, approval or identity than this.

Back to Chris

We started this chapter with a story about a counselee named Chris. Many years later I heard about a public ministry Chris was involved in. He was, in fact, speaking to a massively large crowd in Washington, DC at the National Mall who he sensed and perhaps knew were products of rejection, unwanted by biological parents. Some in the crowd were products of botched abortions. He was announcing at the top of his lungs that while many of those life scenarios might be the case, it did not define who these precious ones were. He then emphasized with every ounce of his being, "God so much wanted you to be born, that how you came into existence is far less important than the fact that He called you into existence. Your heavenly Father gave you birth; you are His wanted, desired and loved creation!"

REFLECT AND DISCUSS

1. Chris received a revelation of who he was. How about you? Do you live in that same revelation?

2. Jeremiah 1 and Ephesians 1 both reveal that God knew you before you were formed in the womb. What does that mean to you and your existence?

I am holy and without blame
before Him.

Ephesians 1:4

I am an heir of God,
a joint heir of Christ.

Romans 8:17

Christ is being formed in me.

Galatians 4:19

I am being conformed into the
likeness of His Son.

Romans 8:29

CHAPTER SEVEN

Created to Be
an Image Bearer

Spiritual identity means we are not what we do or what people say about us. And we are not what we have. We are the beloved daughters and sons of God.
— Henri Nouwen

You have to know your identity. It's the biggest thing in wanting to pursue creative dreams. — Lauren Daigle

When my younger son was living at home with us as an older teenager, he was frequently told by others that he sounded like, looked like and walked like his father. While those observations were not pleasing to him at the time, it was true. Marc, without trying to, bore the image of his biological father. Truthfully, this is not something that we, as sons and daughters, can control due to the fact that God created us to be "image bearers."

In the first chapter of the first book of the Bible, it is revealed that God created man in "his own image, in the image of God he created him; male and female he created them" (Genesis 1:27). David the psalmist wrote, "I praise you, for I am fearfully and wonderfully made" (Psalm 139:14). We were made, created and breathed into that we would bear the image of God, our creator.

Perhaps you have lived life long enough to realize that you did something, said something or thought something which reminded you of one of your parents. You told yourself, "Wow, did that ever sound like my dad." You might have been reminded by a sibling that a certain look, raised eyebrow, laugh or gesticulation reminded them of your mother. It is inescapable, actually. We were created to be image bearers.

For those of you who are fortunate enough to have children of your own, you may already see images in your children that remind you of yourself. It's uncanny how it happens, but it happens for one reason only. When God first created man, He created him to bear an image. The first image we are to bear is the image of our heavenly Father. Make no mistake. Although our created self has the DNA of our family, when traced back to the book of beginnings, Genesis, it is one image and one image only we were fashioned after—the image of God.

It is not an option to be an image bearer, but it is an option as to whose image we bear.

Mere humans

We carry within us the things that have helped to shape us. We can choose to bear the image of a "mere human," or we can choose to move toward that which we were created to be. In I Corinthians 3, Paul tells the Corinthian church that they, too, had a choice. He wrote that who they were acting like, the image they were bearing, was contradicting his desire for them to be persons who "live by the Spirit." He revealed to them they were still acting in a worldly manner due to petty jealousies and the like. His admonishment to them was to stop acting like "mere humans" and start acting like God's temple.

How often have we acted as mere humans with our petty differences, jealousies, offenses or snarky replies? Mere human thoughts are thoughts connected to our earthly existence which do not reflect God's kingdom on earth. Mere human thoughts are self-centered, self-absorbed and self-protecting. These thoughts stem from our minds and not our spirits. They are full of earthly wisdom and bear the fruit of that wisdom. (See James 3:13-16.)

But wisdom generated from above, heavenly wisdom, is "pure, then peace-loving, considerate, submissive, full of mercy and good fruit, impartial and sincere" (James 3:17). The fruit of heavenly wisdom is peace and a harvest of righteousness. (See James 3:18.) Can we comprehend there is a better way, a better foundation, a better image to bear and a better identity to pursue than that which we have followed or have been pursuing?

Going deeper, Paul began talking about the foundation the Galatians were laying for their lives. He told them there were foolish builders and wise builders. He taught them to realize that a foundation built on "gold, silver, costly stones, wood, hay or straw" will be tested. If it is burned up, Paul wrote, the builder will suffer loss. Then he revealed that a true foundation built on Jesus Christ would only be purified if it met with fire.

Paul wrote a key verse regarding the foundation of our identity. He said, "Don't you know that you yourselves are God's temple and that God's Spirit dwells in your midst?" (I Corinthians 3:16)

Definition of identity

It is about time we provide a definition to what we are discussing. The dictionary states that *identity* is "the condition of being oneself, and not another. The condition or character as to who a person or what a thing is; the qualities of belief...that distinguish or identify a person."[1]

For our purposes, the definition we will use in this book is a bit different. Our definition must reflect Someone far superior to us as human beings. It must reflect Someone whose image is eternal and of worth to bear. This identity must reflect the image of the one and only God and the character of His one and only Son, Jesus Christ. Further and finally, the Holy Spirit of God must dwell within the spirit of the person who claims this identity as his or hers.

Here is our definition of identity: *To know who we are and whose we are in bearing the image, the heart and character of our Creator.*

There is nothing religious about this definition; it is fully relational. It is an identity that relates to the Triune God, the One who created identity through His very own work in creation. To bear the image of the One who created us can never be accomplished by mere human thought, balance, personal effort, blood, sweat or tears. It is not accomplished by human effort at all. It is received. An unworthy human vessel is baptized in the love of God, the truth of God, the Spirit of God and the character of God in order to reveal the image of God.

Unknown and undefined by so many

Long before I started to work on this book, I was speaking on the subject of identity and reading books and articles on the subject of identity. I found myself asking everyone who was willing to answer my questions how they would define their personal sense of identity. Among those who responded, most wrote about their personal testimony or their life-compelling thoughts and passions. Few actually understood what identity was or how to write about it. I found that odd. I had assumed that everyone knew where they found their personal sense of worth and identity. I also found it interesting that even believing Christians did not have a fulfilled sense of identity as we define identity: *to know who we are and whose we are in bearing the image and character of our Creator.* That being the case and a surprise to me, what was I to do?

Receiving this identity

I once heard someone ask, "If our identity is connected to what we do, then when we do more, are we more?" Or said a different way: if our identity is connected to our intelligence, then do those who possess a higher IQ also possess a greater, more actualized identity? And, if our identity is connected to our resources, do those who make millions of dollars possess a superior sense of identity?

Obviously, the answer to the above questions is "no." Those who are building their identity on these capacities or beliefs will one day suffer loss. The consequence will also be the loss of their identity. This could be why far too many Hollywood actors and actresses end their lives prematurely through suicide even when they have fame, fortune and notoriety. It is why billionaires are not necessarily fulfilled or happy, despite their billions.

Famous people struggle too

Wikipedia lists over 250 world-famous persons who committed suicide in the 21st century. According to a 2014 study by University of Sydney psychology professor Dianna Kenny, of 12,665 musicians and stars who died between 1950 and June 2014, the chances of famous musicians and rock stars dying from unnatural causes are five to ten times greater than the general population. She found that pop and rock stars die up to twenty-five years younger than average people.[2]

When our art is solely based on our human effort to find identity, notoriety, personal worth and value, then when we are no longer producing art or our art is no longer receiving the attention of significant others or being adored by the masses, we can lose our identity, our self-worth or even our reason for living.

Famous author Henri Nouwen once said concerning success, popularity and power,

"Over the years, I have come to realize that the greatest trap in our life is not success, popularity, or power, but self-rejection. Success, popularity, and power can indeed present a great temptation, but their seductive quality often comes from the way they are part of the much larger temptation to self-rejection. When we have come to believe in the voices that call us worthless and unlovable, then success, popularity, and power are easily perceived as attractive solutions. The real trap, however, is self-rejection. As soon as someone accuses me or criticizes me, as soon as I am rejected, left alone, or abandoned, I find myself thinking, 'Well, that proves once again that I am nobody.' ... [My dark side says,] I am no good.... I deserve to be pushed aside, forgotten, rejected, and abandoned. Self-rejection is the greatest enemy of the spiritual life because it contradicts the sacred voice that calls us the 'Beloved.' Being the Beloved constitutes the core truth of our existence."[3]

A harrowing story of loss[4]

Henri Nouwen was onto something. That "something" plays out in the story I am about to share with you.

His suicide note partly read, "It's better to burn out than fade away." He had become a high school dropout two weeks before graduation. Kurt Cobain was born February 1967 in Aberdeen, Washington. At age nine his parents divorced and he became a recluse, retreating to his bedroom. As his parents found new partners, he felt forgotten and alone. He was bullied in school because he had no interest in sports.

Kurt played in numerous garage bands until putting together the group Nirvana in 1987. Their debut album, *Bleach*, would go diamond and sell over two million copies. Kurt gained lots of attention, critics and admirers through his candid lyrics and songs like "Hate Myself and Want to Die."

As he grew in fame, Kurt become a heavy drug user. Substantial touring took its toll on Cobain and in 1993 he suffered an overdose in New York City. He would overdose again in March of 1994. Briefly he went in and out of rehabilitation centers but did not seem to stick with any level of sobriety. On April 8, 1994, Cobain's body was discovered in his home with a self-inflicted gunshot wound and a suicide note. He was only twenty-seven.

Cobain was one of those musicians whose life grows larger after death. There were tens of thousands of reported mourners around the world. Some would go on to do what he did and commit suicide while listening to his music.

This loss of life and complete loss of identity seems to connect with the findings mentioned above concerning premature unnatural deaths among such famous musicians and people.

Desire the image of Christ

Jesus was surrounded by deception, by false prophets, by religious ones who had selfish goals in mind, by political ones, by criminals and by many persons who only wanted nothing more than a miracle from Him. How did He handle all this pressure and yet maintain who He was?

One day the disciples were discussing among themselves with Jesus present what it must be like to see God, the Father. Jesus then began telling them that He needed to go away and they were unable to come with Him. He revealed that He was going to prepare a place where they could come. Then Thomas asked Him, "How can we know this way?" Jesus said these wonderful words in reply: "I am the way and the truth and the life. No one comes to the Father except through me." He added, "If you really knew me, you would know my Father as well" (John 14:5-7).

The disciple Philip then inquired of Jesus to show them the Father. Jesus' reply was pretty firm. "Don't you know me, Philip, even after I have been among you such a long time? Anyone who has seen me has seen the Father…. I am in the Father and the Father is in me" (John 14:9, 11). From this dialogue, we are reminded that there was only one image the Son was reflecting—the Father.

Paul the Apostle confirms Jesus' words when he writes, "He [Jesus] is the image of the invisible God, the firstborn over all creation" (Colossians 1:15). Perhaps the disciples struggled to comprehend this level of identity building, but Paul did not. Paul was a trained Pharisee and he understood the dilemma of having your security, your esteem, your image and your identity built within a religious system that failed to show him who he really was.

For Paul, it took an encounter with Jesus on the road to Damascus where he received a vision and heard the voice of Jesus for himself. Just after this amazing and personal encounter, the Lord said to Ananias, another disciple, concerning Saul, "This man is my chosen instrument to carry **my name** before the Gentiles and their kings" (Acts 9:15, emphasis mine).

Wow, a voice from heaven saying that Saul, who would be renamed to Paul the Apostle, would be set apart to "carry my name." What name? The name of Jesus. What did that name represent? The name of the One whose image you, Paul, are going to reflect to the whole Gentile world! God literally knocked Saul off his feet, revealed Himself to him and then sent him to carry His name, the name of the Father, the Son and the Holy Spirit.

Up to this point in time, Saul was carrying his given name and his authority in his Pharisaical beliefs. While this character was powerful and ended the lives of Christians, God had a different name, different mission and different identity for Saul. He would become Paul, a chosen vessel that would carry a much more powerful name, mission and identity.

We carry that name today as well. This name is above every other name on this earth. This name represents the image of our God within us. Our given name can do none of these things.

My name vs. His name

My last name is a tough one. I am told it is of Ukrainian descent. It is pronounced Pro-kop-chak. It's simple when broken down into three syllables. It is so often misspelled. You would laugh out loud at how some of my mail is actually addressed: Steve Perkupcha, Steve Percopcheck and even Steve Porkchop. It's embarrassing at times. But my last name is **not** who I am. That name can save no one. That name has no power, no capacity to do anything for anyone.

Jesus has always known my name. He has never mis-spelled my name or made fun of it. He has never ridiculed my name. In His creation of me, it has been His desire to place His name within me so that I know Him and function out of that personal relationship, knowledge and spiritual connection with Him.

He knows your name, too. He knew you before you were in the womb of your mother. He calls you by name. He loves your name, the sound of your name, the sound of your voice, because He loves you. Your name represents your existence on the earth and His call to you to follow Him. Just as the disciples questioned, He wants to show you Himself and show you His Father. Just like Paul, He has chosen you to carry His name, His identity and who He is to the world around you. Your name will save no one, but His name lived through you can touch many with His love.

Let's complete this chapter with three amazing scriptures that drive home the truth we have been discussing. As you read them, receive them into your spirit. Let them go beyond your history, your family line and your family name. Let them take you to that place of identity that you have only dreamed of connecting with. (The emphasis in these verses is mine.)

Romans 8:29 – "For those God foreknew he also pre-destined to be **conformed to the likeness of his Son...**"

I Corinthians 15:49 – "And just as we have borne the likeness of the earthly man, **so shall we bear the likeness of the man from heaven.**"

II Corinthians 3:18 – "And we, who with unveiled faces all **reflect the Lord's glory, are being transformed into his likeness** with ever-increasing glory, which comes from the Lord who is the Spirit."

If you can think of the last name of the wealthiest person or the most well-known person on earth today, that name does not carry an ounce of identity for you. That name cannot conform you to any good image. That name will not supply a single fraction of transformation in your life, even if you were related to or best friends with that person.

There is only one name, one likeness, one image, one glory and one identity to reflect: Jesus.

REFLECT AND DISCUSS

1. Can you list some ways in which you recognize that you are an image bearer of your parents?

2. How do you identify with the phrase "an unworthy, human vessel"?

3. How are you growing in your reflection of the image of Christ, His name vs. your name?

ENDNOTES

1. www.dictionary.com.

2. Rob Taylor, "The 27 Club Is a Myth, but Rock Stars Do Die Younger," *Wall Street Journal*, October 28, 2014, https://www.wsj.com/articles/the-27-club-is-a-myth-but-rock-stars-do-die-younger-1414490051?mod=WSJ_hp_EditorsPicks.

3. Henri J. M. Nouwen, *You Are the Beloved: Daily Meditations for Spiritual Living* (New York: Convergent Books, 2017).

4. Sal Bono, "The True Story of Nirvana Frontman Kurt Cobain," *Inside Edition*, last modified April 2, 2019, https://www.insideedition.com/true-story-nirvana-frontman-kurt-cobain-51701.

I am an heir, a son of God.

Galatians 4:7

I am a new creature in Christ.

II Corinthians 5:17

Jesus has overcome the world
and I am an overcomer.

John 16:33

I am partaker of the divine
nature of God.

II Peter 1:4

CHAPTER EIGHT

Testing Our Identity

Our scars make us who we are. Wear them proudly, and move forward. — Jane Linfoot, *The Little Wedding Shop by the Sea*

*My very identity as a soldier came to an abrupt end.
I'd been soldiering as long as I'd been shaving.
Suddenly I'd been told I could no longer soldier, and it felt
as though no one really cared if I ever shaved again.*
— Stanley A. McChrystal

One of the biggest tests of our identity is the test of approval from others. We long for positive attention to justify our very existence. But what if it could be different, far different?

Jesus had just been baptized in the Jordan River, filled with the Spirit of God and spoken over by His heavenly Father who called Jesus His beloved Son. Jesus knew who His Father was and therefore knew who He was as well. (See John 5:17-48.) Almost immediately following this heavenly affirmation comes a repeated test of His identity.

From the Jordan River, Jesus is led by the Spirit to the desert, where He will be tested and tempted for forty days by the devil. The first words out of the devil's mouth were, "If you are the Son of God…" This phrase is repeated several times. We might paraphrase this line of questioning by saying, "So, you think you know who you are; let's see about that…" or, "If your identity is in the One you say it is, then…"

We now see the importance of the words that Jesus' Father spoke over Him while in the Jordan River. Jesus now faced the biggest test of His miraculous abilities, His very life, and His purpose for coming to earth. Jesus passed the tests. In the end He told the devil, "Away from me, Satan! For it is written: 'Worship the Lord your God and serve him only'" (Matthew 4:10).

Jesus would not worship the devil, nor be tempted to worship Himself. Can we pass these tests of identity when the evil one lies to us with a similar phrase like, "Who do you think you are?" or "So, you're claiming your identity in Christ; we'll see about that." Tests are just that: a test. They are not necessarily life or death, but if we do not know who we are and our identity is not solidly found within the Father's love for us, then we most likely will not pass the test of identity.

When we do pass, we can be assured there will be another test forthcoming. The devil is relentless when it comes to attacking us in this manner. Why? If he can get us to doubt our identity in God's love and approval, then he can also get us to doubt our salvation, our relationship with God or whether or not we are loved by God.

Peter wrote it this way: "But you are not like that, for *you are* a chosen people. *You are* royal priests, a holy nation, *God's own possession.* As a result, you can show others the goodness of God, for he called you out of the darkness into wonderful light" (I Peter 2:10 NLT, emphasis mine).

Pharisees recognized Jesus' identity

I love the expression of the Pharisees when they addressed Jesus in Mark 12:14, "Teacher, we know that you are a man of integrity. You aren't swayed by others, because you pay no attention to who they are; but you teach the way of God in accordance with the truth." Of course, their words are a bit of a setup because they would try to trap Him in their next question. But they did speak truth. Jesus was not "swayed." He did not need to "pay… attention" to others because He knew whose He was.

When you look in the mirror, what do you see? Do you see one who is not swayed and is not constantly looking for the approval of men, like Jesus? Do you see the one who can pass the tests of identity? Let me share with you four revelations that are needed to pass those tests.

The four revelations

Each of us need these four revelations in our lives in order to continue the process of understanding our identity. I call them revelations because we do not reason our way into these truths. It is not a matter of mind over will. They are revelations because they come from the Spirit of God to our spirit.

Romans 8 gives us insight into this life-giving concept. Romans 8:5 reveals that if we live according to the flesh, our minds will be set on the flesh and what the flesh desires (earthly thoughts, pleasures, self-centered cravings). But, if we live according to the Spirit and desire what the Spirit of God desires, our minds will be "governed" by the Spirit of God. The author continues to write that the mind that is governed by the flesh is death-filled, but the mind that is governed by the Spirit is filled with "life and peace."

1. We are heirs, the children of God

If the Spirit of God dwells in us, then we are filled with what the Scriptures reveal *is the Spirit that "gives life."* Further, in Romans 8:16 we are spoken over with these deeply compelling words: "The Spirit himself testifies with our spirit that we are God's children. Now if we are children, then we are heirs—heirs of God and co-heirs with Christ."

This scriptural premise depicts the first revelation. We know this by revelation because this revelation is given to us *from our spirit to our mind and not from our mind to our spirit.*

2. We are a new creation

II Corinthians 5:17 is revelation when it comes to our new self: "Therefore, if anyone is in Christ, the new creation has come: The old has gone, the new is here!" You are a new creation in Christ. A new creation has a newly developing mind because the Spirit of Christ is renewing our mind. Elsewhere in Corinthians we are told that we have the mind of Christ. (See I Corinthians 2:16.) To have the mind of Christ is a revelation because we are thinking His thoughts and then speaking His words from our spirit. It is similar to what Jesus so often stated when He said that He only spoke what the Father revealed to Him.

I was in my counseling office one day, basically reprimanding a counselee for not completing his reading assignments, when I heard the voice of the Spirit say, "Ask him if he struggles with reading." I thought, "What? Who can't read in this day and age?" But I obeyed and asked Mike if he struggled with reading. Immediately he dropped his head as if to say, "You found me out." He then told me he was unable to read and could barely write. It was the Spirit of God who revealed that word of knowledge to me.

We have the mind of Christ. By revelation, we can hear and speak His mind.

3. We are overcomers

Jesus told us that in this world we would have trouble and tribulation, but that we were not to be discouraged because He has overcome the world. (See John 16:33.) We are overcomers in Him by revelation!

Further in Romans 12 we are admonished to live life this way: "Hate what is evil; Be devoted to one another; Love one another; …be patient, be joyful, be faithful in prayer, practice hospitality, live in harmony with one another, do not repay evil for evil, live at peace with everyone, do not take revenge and overcome evil with good." I am not sure how any of us think we can live this life without God's presence and His identity in our lives. Living in a self-sacrificing way can only be done by the revelation that we are overcomers.

Mother Teresa was once asked by journalists if she ever felt like a failure. Her answer to them was by revelation. She said, "No, because I am not trying to be a success, only obedient." Mother Teresa was not a failure, nor did she describe herself as one; she was an overcomer. She understood revelation number three and walked it out on a daily basis. This was the only way one could continue to reach the lives she was reaching. "This is love for God: to obey his commands…for everyone born of God overcomes the world… Who is it that overcomes the world? Only he who believes that Jesus is the Son of God" (I John 5:3, 4).

4. The purpose of identity is not about me

Tying this all together is revelation number four. It is the "why" of identity. For God to reveal this revelation to us, our flesh must get out of the way. We need to receive a revelation of why He chooses to live within us. He chooses this path in order to equip us to live out His story on the earth for the season that we exist on this earth.

Acts 17 states, "The God who made the world and everything in it is the Lord of heaven and earth and does not live in temples built by hands. And he is not served by human hands, as if he needed anything, because he himself gives all men life and breath and everything else. From one man he made every nation of men, that they should inhabit the whole earth; *and he determined the times set for them and the exact places where they should live*" (Acts 17:24-26; emphasis mine).

God determined your birth for this time and this season. God saved you for this time and this season. God lives in you for this time and this season. You live where you live because He determined the "exact places" for you to live out His story on earth. You could have easily been born an African or a European if you're a North American. You could have been born in the nation of Haiti or He could have placed you in China. It is His determination; it's not yours!

When it's all about us, we can feel free to defend ourselves. We can feel free to live out our life in the way we so determine. If it's about us, we can choose to live in hurt and rejection or simply focus fully on ourselves, our pleasures and our needs. This revelation determines that our lives possess a much higher calling. We become His eyes, His ears, His spokespersons and the evidence of His love to the world around us.

"Therefore I urge you, brothers and sisters, in view of God's mercy, to offer your bodies as a living sacrifice, holy and pleasing to God—this is your true and proper worship. Do not conform to the pattern of this world, but be transformed by the renewing of your mind" (Romans 12:1, 2).

We are born into self-centeredness. Self-centeredness could be our attempt at preserving who we think we should be, regardless of what others think about us. However, the truth of these four revelations will take us far beyond self-filled effort. When we incorporate these four revelations from our spirit, we know our life is not our own. It is for His honor and His glory. We no longer live by life circumstances, but by the revelation that I am His and He is mine.

The revelation of God's Word

Traveling with these four revelations is also the revelation of the Word of God.

I write a weekly blog. One of those blogs was titled, "21 Books You Don't Have to Read." It was basically generated from an article found in *GQ* magazine from 2018. The author identified some amazing books as being no longer necessary to read. The list included books like *The Old Man and the Sea*, *Adventures of Huckleberry Finn* and even *The Lord of the Rings*.

But what really intrigued me in this article was one other book: the Holy Bible. The author stated, "…rated very highly by all the people who supposedly live by it but who in actuality have not read it." Obviously, this was a huge misconception.

I wrote in my blog, "But, if you believe it to be divinely inspired and given to us by the hand of God, then do not forsake it. Do not miss the clear historical facts found in it. Do not miss the giving of the law which helped to bring about purity, cleanliness, integrity *and connection with our Creator.* Do not miss Jesus, the Son of God, in every book of the Bible. Do not miss the true-to-life parables and do not miss the prophecy already fulfilled and yet to be fulfilled."

The Word of God is so much more than a book; it is sixty-six books of congruent, life-giving, faith-building, history-teaching, future-telling, mind-changing, truth-filled counsel and loved-filled affirmations. Check out these words: "Every word of God is flawless; he is a shield to those who take refuge in him" (Proverbs 30:5). And these words, "For the word of God is alive and active. Sharper than any double-edged sword, it penetrates even to dividing souls and spirit, joints and marrow; it judges the thoughts and attitudes of the heart" (Hebrews 4:12).

That last verse saying, "…it penetrates…dividing soul and spirit" describes the revelation of the Word of God, the Bible, in our lives. It is not just a book to place on the shelf and stop reading, for it is never outdated. It is more current than tomorrow's newspaper or news on the internet. It is life-giving, Holy Spirit–inspired application for daily living, and it is life-altering truth.

The proof of that truth is found in Scripture. Catch this from the Gospel of John. "In the beginning was the Word, and the Word was with God, and the Word was God. He was with God from the beginning…. The Word became flesh and made his dwelling among us" (John 1:1, 2). Who is the Word? It is Jesus Christ, the Son of God. He is the Word of Truth. He lived among us and He gave us the Scriptures. They are His words, His revelation, and His inspiration.

Never should we sell this book short. There is more truth in it from the One who is Truth than any academic broadside can reveal, any source of human wisdom can give, or any fortune-teller can foretell.

Yet another truth-filled scripture

I John 4:4 connects to the concepts in this chapter. It provides strength for the pursuit of a healthy identity. It states emphatically what God is trying to say to us as we receive His love and His revelation of identity.

You dear children, are from God and have overcome them, because **the one who is in you is greater than the one who is in the world** (I John 4:4, emphasis mine).

No longer do we need to walk in self-pity. No longer do we need to be a victim of our past or our circumstances. No longer do we need to gather those around ourselves who reinforce whatever it is we are feeling. No longer do we need others to feel sorry for us under any circumstance. We are overcomers who walk in the revelation of His love, acceptance and approval. He is greater in us than all our past, present or future life circumstances.

REFLECT AND DISCUSS

1. Those life-affirming words that the Father spoke over His Son at His baptism are spoken over you as well. What do you hear God saying to you personally?

2. Of the four revelations, which one stands out to you? Which one do you struggle with the most? Which one has been the easiest for you to receive?

3. When you think of the revelation of God's Word to you, what comes to mind?

4. How is I John 4:4 a personal revelation to you?

I am without blemish.

Colossians 1:22

I am reconciled to God.

II Corinthians 5:18

I am the head and not the tail.

Deuteronomy 28:13

I am forgiven.

I John 2:12

CHAPTER NINE

Healing a Damaged Soul's Identity

One of the things about incarceration is that you're deprived. You lose all of your identity, and then it's given back one day, and you're ill-equipped to actually embrace it and work it. — Susan Burton

The truth is, your identity already has been stolen.
— Frank Abagnale

Regardless of what has happened to you in your past, those things do not define who you are today. Your pain-filled memories, your losses, rejections, embarrassments and shame are all but a passing moment in time. They are either moments that fill you with heartache, unforgiveness and bitterness, or they are moments that have worked to create a better you. You have either embraced them as truth and told yourself your worth and value are determined by those things, or you have embraced the experience of them, sought healing, and matured tremendously by allowing them to grow you into a deeper, more forgiving, more grace-filled and more loving person.

You have been given one life to live on this earth. It is up to you how you will live it. If you allow anyone else on earth to determine how you will live, forfeiting your identity to the identity they have determined for you, then you have sold yourself to another. It is God who has given you life and breath, not anyone else.

Every day people are born and every day people die. You have been given a gift of life and it's up to you what you make of it. You can live in history, in the present or in constant hope of a better future.

Forgiveness and identity

If you choose to live in the past, then you most likely are choosing to live in unforgiveness. Unforgiveness gives birth to brokenness, being stuck in life, the loss of freedom, physical illnesses, depression, bitterness, anger, self-pity, self-torment, and the like. Living in unforgiveness is an anguishing way to live. It holds us in bondage to others. I believe it was author and speaker Joyce Meyer who said that holding on to unforgiveness is like drinking poison in the hope that the one who you cannot forgive dies. But the poison only hurts you. Unforgiveness brings certain death to any sense of wholeness and identity.

Counselees would often say to me, "You have no idea what I have been through." They were right. But you will not move forward if you stick with that excuse. When you live life in the "You have no idea what I have been through" mode, you will remain stuck in your history. It is not always about what we have been through; it's about who He is in you for yesterday, today and tomorrow. It's about how those things you experienced have forced growth in your life.

Does that mean we are in denial of our past? No, it does not. But if you are constantly looking back, you will eventually run into something, and it will hurt.

I live in a farming community in Pennsylvania. Farmers work the soil year after year with their tractors and attached implements. A farmer once told me that when you plow the field, you need to find an object on the opposite end of the field and drive straight towards it, not taking your eye off the object. In that way, your first furrow will be straight and you will have a pattern to follow. But if you take your eye off the fence post or tree and look back at where you have been, your tractor will almost positively stray.

You can be fifty, sixty or seventy years old and still be looking back. You can die looking back. As long as we are looking in the rearview mirror, it will be impossible to move forward in great measure. Your identity is not and will never be found in your history.

Waiting for an apology

If you are waiting for an apology from that person who hurt you, you might have to wait all your life. That confession may never come. Those tears of sorrow for hurting you might never surface. Then what? If you keep waiting, placing your life on hold, you have become a captive of the person or persons who hurt you. You have empowered them to control your life and your emotions. You have made them more powerful than yourself and more powerful than God. You are allowing them to determine who you are and what you are.

Jesus is as concerned about your future as He is your past. The Holy Spirit desires to move you on. No one created by God was designed to live life looking backwards, constantly filtering everything that happens today through what happened yesterday.

When you know God's forgiveness through His Son's death on the cross, you will no longer need to wait for an apology. You will no longer be stuck in history. You will no longer have a bottomless hole that cannot be filled and you will no longer be controlled by another person.

How does forgiveness occur?

Jesus straightforwardly said we were to forgive as we have been forgiven. Have you ever needed forgiveness? How many persons have you hurt? Every one of us is in desperate need of forgiveness. How then do we hold others captive with unforgiveness?

Here is the good news: from the cross Jesus said, "I forgive you." That's it, period, done deal, no qualifiers and no "buts." It is forgiveness without condition. Let's take a closer look at that forgiveness through a real-life story.

Corrie ten Boom once said, "Forgiveness is an act of the will, and the will can function regardless of the temperature of the heart."

Corrie's story is a harrowing one. Corrie was born April 15, 1892. She was a Dutch watchmaker, the daughter of a watchmaker from Amsterdam, Netherlands. She and her family were hiding Jews in order to help them escape the Nazi Holocaust during World War II. Her family was found out and she was arrested and sent to Ravensbruck concentration camp. Her book *The Hiding Place*[1] is a biography that tells the story of her amazing life.

Corrie tells a story after her release from the camp in which she met one of her Nazi guards face-to-face following a speaking engagement. Her story illustrates forgiveness in a very powerful way.

"It was in a church in Munich that I saw him—a balding, heavyset man in a gray overcoat, a brown felt hat clutched between his hands. People were filing out of the basement room where I had just spoken, moving along the rows of wooden chairs to the door at the rear. It was 1947 and I had come from Holland to defeated Germany with the message that God forgives. It was the truth they needed most to hear in that bitter, bombed-out land, and I gave them my favorite mental picture."[2]

What Corrie really saw was not a man in a gray overcoat, but a man in a blue uniform and a visored cap with its skull and crossbones. She immediately felt the shame of walking past this man naked in a huge room with piles of shoes and clothing discarded in the center of the space.

This man had been a guard at Ravensbruck concentration camp where Corrie and her sister were imprisoned.

Corrie writes, "Now he was in front of me, hand thrust out: 'A fine message, *Fräulein*! How good it is to know that, as you say, all our sins are at the bottom of the sea!'"[3]

She realized she was standing in front of one of her guards from the concentration camp, but he did not remember who she was. However, Corrie remembered him and his leather crop swinging from his belt. Standing in front of him, she felt as though her blood was frozen.

He went on to explain that since his time at Ravensbruck he had become a Christian. He shared with her that he now knew God's forgiveness for the many cruel things he had inflicted on people. He held out his hand and asked "Fräulein" Corrie ten Boom if she would also forgive him.

"And I stood there—I whose sins had to again and again be forgiven—and could not forgive. Betsie [her sister] had died in that place—could he erase her slow terrible death simply for the asking?"[4]

Corrie knew she had to forgive this man because she also knew that the Scripture says, "If you do not forgive men their trespasses, neither will your Father in heaven forgive your trespasses."

Corrie shares, "I knew it not only as a commandment of God, but as a daily experience. Since the end of the war I had had a home in Holland for victims of Nazi brutality. Those who were able to forgive their former enemies were able also to return to the outside world and rebuild their lives, no matter what the physical scars. Those who nursed their bitterness remained invalids. It was as simple and as horrible as that."[5]

Finally, through an act of her will she raised her hand and placed it into the hand that was stretched out toward her. She looked into her former enemy's eyes and said, "I forgive you, brother, with all my heart!"

She continues to explain: "For a long moment we grasped each other's hands, the former guard and the former prisoner. I had never known God's love so intensely, as I did then."[6]

True forgiveness is not just releasing someone. True forgiveness is not asking God to "go after" someone so you don't have to. True forgiveness is not a denial of justice. When we do not forgive, we are actually crying out to God for our own retribution.

The Old Testament atonement

The Old Testament law required the shedding of blood of bulls, goats, lambs and doves. That offering of the high priest on the altar of sacrifice provided atonement for the sin of the people. Atonement was not forgiveness; it was a covering up of sin, so to speak. However, throughout the Old Testament there was a foretelling of the One who would take away the sins of the world forever, the final sacrificial Lamb of God. (See Isaiah 53.)

The book of Hebrews explains about the Law: "In fact, the law requires that nearly everything be cleansed with blood, and without the shedding of blood there is no forgiveness" (Hebrews 9:22).

Ephesians 1:7 states, "In him we have redemption through his blood, the forgiveness of sins."

We are forgiven of past, present and future sin by the sacrifice of Jesus on the cross. He freely placed Himself there.

One of my favorite scenes in Mel Gibson's movie *The Passion of the Christ* is when Jesus and the Roman soldiers finally reach the top of the hill called Golgotha. The Roman soldiers do not force Jesus on the cross. He does not try to run from the cross, but rather He willingly lays Himself on the rough, wooden cross. He knows it is His calling to die a sacrificial death for the final atonement of the sins of the world. There would be no more need to sacrifice animals; He would be the final sacrificial Lamb of God. (See John 1:29 and I Corinthians 5:7.) With this came forgiveness for every life ever lived for over two thousand years.

Jesus chose to lay His life down as a ransom for my sin and your sin. He chose to forgive us and never bring up our sin again. Even when we fall short of His ideal for us, we can come to Him with a sincere heart and confess our sin. When we do so, we are totally, unreservedly forgiven.

A completely new view from heaven

Colossians says it this way: "Once you were alienated from God and were enemies in your minds because of your evil behavior. But now he has reconciled you by Christ's physical body through death to **present you holy in his sight, without blemish and free from accusation**—if you continue in your faith, established and firm, not moved from the hope held out in the gospel" (Colossians 1:21-23, emphasis mine).

Once again, the Word of God confirms that it is not what we can do, but what He has already done for us. We were far from God and our identity was lost in so many unmentionable ways. We were living a life in which we acted as enemies of God, perhaps even cursing His name. But then through His sacrifice on the cross, He presents us holy, without blemish and free from accusation!

Granted, we do not always feel holy or think holy thoughts, but that is how God sees us. For most of us, when looking in the mirror, we see all our blemishes, but He does not. Lastly, we are free of the demeaning voice of the accuser, the devil.

Blemishes

One day my wife, Mary, who is a registered nurse, came home from work with black spots under each of her eyes. I questioned her about what could have happened. She told me, "Oh, you know all those white spots, age marks, I had under my eyes? Well, I had the doctor burn them off." I told her I had never seen any white spots but that those black spots were far worse.

Mary saw those white spots every time she looked in the mirror. Not everyone noticed them, not even her husband, but she did. We tend to look at a picture of ourselves and see blemishes: the crooked nose, the mole, the scar or the receding hair line. The same is true of our emotional blemishes and past sins. We "see" and recall our selfish behavior, our sinful sexual exploits and our insecurities. The evil one even reminds us of them.

I was seated at my grandson's graduation from kindergarten in a small school auditorium. A young active boy in the seat in front of me turned around in boredom, looked at me and said out loud, "You have no eyebrows!" He caught me so off guard that I wanted to respond, "Yeah, well you have no manners," but I did not; I just smiled at him. The truth is, I do have eyebrows even though they are gray and very faint. Well, I now know about one more of my imperfections, thanks to this observant little boy.

But here is the really good news: those verses in Colossians tell us that those blemishes are no longer a part of us, we have been made holy, and we cannot be accused any longer. We have been forgiven and we are free.

This is the line we started chapter nine with: regardless of what has happened to you in your past, those things do not define who you are today. Here is why: we are forgiven, off the hook, released, reconciled, brought back into right standing with God (redemption) through His Son. Our identity is intact as long as it is centered in Him.

We are primarily spirit

We are primarily spiritual beings, not just physical beings or sexual beings. I Thessalonians 5:23 says, "May your whole **spirit, soul and body** be kept blameless at the coming of our Lord Jesus Christ." Housed within our body is our soul: our mind, will and emotions. But the eternal part, the primary part of us, is our spirit.

All too often we are told our feelings are most important. They are not. Our feelings are subject to our thoughts. If I tell you a joke and you do not think it's funny, you will not have the feeling or emotional response of laughter. If you do think it's funny, your reaction will be to laugh. Our feelings are a result of or a reaction to our thoughts.

Our thoughts are a result of our beliefs. If we believe it is right to stop at red lights, then we will think thoughts that align with that belief and, finally, we will choose the action of stopping at the red light.

So, when breaking identity connections or beliefs that are not in line with God's truth for us, He changes our beliefs by His Spirit speaking to our spirit. How does that occur? Perhaps as we read through the Bible, we come across a truth that we were unaware of. By the conviction of the Spirit, we ask God to change our belief to His belief. Or perhaps a message we hear from a Sunday morning worship service changes a thought. Perhaps a friend challenges us and our belief with a new truth-filled concept to consider.

Each of us has changing beliefs. These changes happen more frequently than we might realize. For example, if we want our actions to change, our beliefs must change first. Just because we feel something deeply, it does not mean that it is truth. All too often in the counseling room I would hear something like this: "I am aware that the Bible says such and such, but how could something that feels this good be so wrong?"

The counselee in this example seems to know the truth of the Bible, but overrides the truth with what his feelings dictate. In other words, knowing a certain behavior is wrong, he justifies it by how he feels. This line of thinking will never make a wrong right or create positive or lasting change.

Another example: just because I become extremely angry and feel like hurting someone, should I act upon that feeling? In the same way, if I feel as though I have no worth or no value and I am struggling to find my identity, should I act on those feelings and believe them, making them more powerful than truth?

Breaking identity attachments

A positive, relational example of an identity connection is found in I Samuel 18:1, "After David had finished talking with Saul, Jonathan became one in spirit with David and he loved him as himself." In this example, there was a knitting together of two lives for a common purpose, a common goal. We each have the capacity to align our mind, our will, our emotions and our spirit with others who desire the same.

Romans 12:5 tells us those who are in Christ are many and yet we form one body and that each member of this body belongs to the others. I Corinthians 12:26 gives another example, as Paul writes that when one member in the body suffers or rejoices, we each suffer or rejoice together.

Godly and ungodly connections

There are two types of human connections: godly, as well as ungodly. We can bond with the good—the godly—and with the ungodly. Paul states in I Corinthians 15:33, "Do not be misled: 'Bad company corrupts good character.'" (See also Proverbs 22:24, 25.)

This attachment with one another is a connection God created in each of us in order to care for, minister to, be a friend with, counsel, employ, be employed and be married. We are not islands. Within our relationships we are honestly walking out Romans 12:10, "Be devoted to one another in brotherly love. Honor one another above yourselves." When this love and honor occurs, we are responding as Jesus asked us to respond to each other; it is a positive, healthy, godly soul connection.

There is, however, a negative, ungodly, and unhealthy soul connection that each of us encounters and must be aware of. Galatians 5:15 warns, "If you keep on biting and devouring each other, watch out or you will be destroyed by each other." The same soul connection that carries love can carry destruction and injury.

Unequally yoked

The Bible tells us to not be unequally yoked together with unbelievers (II Corinthians 6:14). Picture cattle yoked together; what one does, so does the other. We are told in Scripture to sever these ties, come out from among them and be separate (II Corinthians 6:17). Why? Because there is a potential human bonding that takes place.

Put a newborn child against a mother's breast, skin-to-skin, and chemicals in the brain will be released that cause the mother and the child to bond together. Put pornography before your eyes and those same chemicals will be released that cause extremely negative bonding. Have an illicit sexual affair and there will not only be a chemical exchange, but an ungodly bonding soul-to-soul exchange.

God knew we could bond to these images and so He told us to not make for ourselves any carved image, to not bow down to them or serve them. God knew about the bonding factor with images and false gods. There is only one image of God we are to bond to. That image is of His Son, Jesus.

Healthy marriage bonds

We are created to be joined, bonded together, soul and spirit in the marriage union. God's Word tells us, "…a man shall leave his father and mother and cleave [be bonded to, be joined to, be cemented to] his wife and be **one flesh**" (Genesis 2:24, emphasis mine). In Ephesians 5:31 the Bible says, "For this reason a man will leave his father and mother and be united to his wife, and the two will become one flesh."

This follows Jesus' example in John 14:10, "I am in the Father, and [the] Father is in me" and John 10:30, "I and the Father are one." Jesus concludes this picture of oneness, of joining our spirit, with His words in John 14:20 which reads, "I am in my Father, and you are in me, and I am in you." There is no better picture of godly bonding.

Ungodly human connections

I Corinthians 6:15-17 reveals there can be a flesh-to-flesh connection, there can be a soul-to-soul connection and there can be a spirit-to-spirit connection.

Do you not know that your bodies are members of Christ himself? Shall I then take the members of Christ and unite them with a prostitute? Never! Do you not know that he who unites himself with a prostitute is one with her in body? For it is said, "The two will become one flesh." But he who unites himself with the Lord is one with him in spirit.

In this identity connection there is an ungodly uniting. It is why evil occult groups always include human blood or animal blood sacrifice in their ceremonies. The Bible tells us that the life is in the blood (Leviticus 17:14) and we are commanded to not drink or eat the blood. The blood provided the strongest tie or connection. We are to unite with God and not to unite with ungodly one-flesh connections.

Where we have or have had these types of soul connections, there needs to be a severing which includes confession, repentance, renouncing and blessing. All of these ungodly connections affect our present life beliefs, thoughts, emotions, actions and identities.

Steps to healing

Wherever there was an alignment of wills, an agreement of emotions, a sexual connection, an inordinate life-to-life connection, we need to ask our heavenly Father to reveal these connections to us in listening prayer. Ask Jesus to reveal any spirit, soul and body connections that are still holding on to you. These are connections that you know you had or perhaps no longer remember that you had, but Jesus will show you or reveal them to you.

As these areas are identified, repent of your part, your alignment and agreement with these ungodly connections. Ask God for forgiveness of these things and thank Him for doing so.

Once repented of, ask Jesus to take back, remove and disconnect these attachments, alignments and agreements by the power of His shed blood and the placing of His cross between you and the person you were connected to.

Bind any powers of darkness connected person-to-person coming from this ungodly soul connection.

Ask Holy Spirit to fill the void with His presence, His healing, His freedom and His identity.

A sample prayer to help walk you through these steps

Father, I place (name the person) under the authority of Jesus Christ and I ask You, Jesus, to completely sever the ungodly spirit, soul and body connections between them and me. I ask you, Jesus, to remove from me any and all connections and return them to (name the person). I declare a broken, severed alignment between us in Jesus' name. By faith I place the cross of Jesus and His shed blood between us. It is the cross and Your shed blood that has the power to sever this ungodly connection.

Also, I take authority over any demonic connection and power linked to and through this person. I command you to leave this cleansed vessel without harm and to go where Jesus sends you. I release any rights that the evil one had in this soul connection and I prohibit any evil spirit from damaging myself or the other party.

Now I ask you, Holy Spirit, to fill this void in my life with your love, your power and your freedom from each and every ungodly soul connection, in Jesus' name.

Heavenly Father, I pray that You break every yoke, every connection, all unforgiveness and every ungodly attachment found within any relationship past and present and make me aware of any ungodly alignments the enemy of my soul would attempt to bring to me in the future. In Jesus' name, Amen.

The shedding of Christ's blood cleanses us from the sin connections of our past, our present and our future. It is His blood that was required as the final sacrificed Lamb. No more shedding of blood for sin or ungodly soul connections is needed. Jesus has come to bring us freedom from everything the enemy of our souls meant to bind us with. As Galatians 5:1 states, "It is for freedom that Christ has set us free."

In the next chapter we will consider a unique area of identity attachments: sexual identity attachments.

REFLECT AND DISCUSS

1. What are your thoughts on the statement that your history or your hurts from the past do not define who you are today?

2. Have you thought of anyone you have not forgiven? How does this affect your relationship with that person? How can you move toward forgiveness?

3. What blemishes do you see when you look in the mirror? What blemishes does the evil one remind you of regularly?

4. How have you been able to identify soul connections affecting your personal worth and identity?

ENDNOTES

1. Corrie ten Boom, *The Hiding Place* (New York: Bantam Books, 1974).

2–6. Corrie ten Boom, "I'm Still Learning to Forgive." *Guideposts* (Carmel, NY: Guideposts Associates, Inc., 1972).

I am redeemed from
the curse of the law.

Galatians 3:13

For freedom Christ has set me free.

Galatians 5:1

I have the mind of Christ.

I Corinthians 2:16

I am kept by God's power.

I Peter 1:5

I am in Christ Jesus by God's act.

I Corinthians 1:30

PART 3: SEXUAL IDENTITY
CHAPTER TEN

Sexual Brokenness

When I discover who I am, I'll be free.
— Ralph Ellison, *Invisible Man*

The true identity theft is not financial. It's not in cyber-space. It's spiritual. It's been taken. — Stephen Covey

Note: This chapter and the next are dedicated to our struggle with sexual brokenness. I encourage you not to skip these chapters, as our sexuality is a significant part of who we are as God's creation.

When I was a child, Ricky and Lucy, a married couple on a popular television show called *I Love Lucy*, slept in separate single beds. Now, we are hard-pressed to find any television show or movie that depicts God's covenant of marriage and honors His sexual boundaries. Even if the program rating does not allow sex to be shown, it is often implied.

In my brief lifetime, sex has turned into something casual that does not require commitment. Many different sexually transmitted diseases have spread because our culture has taken sex outside of marriage and pushed back God's boundaries for sex as unobtainable, prudish and rather old-fashioned.

The sad thing is that I have my own generation to blame for this moral decline. It was my generation from the '60s and

'70s that pushed the envelope for sexual freedoms. Drugs and sex were taken "out of the shadows" and indulged in openly at rock concerts in the name of peace, love and freedom. We said it was our right to disobey the law. We insisted that it would hurt no one.

As teenagers and twenty-somethings, we spread our wings and rebelled against our parents. We broke the only commandment that ends with a promise, to obey your parents, and we have been reaping the seeds sown ever since. We opened the door to sexual brokenness, legalized abortion and the breakdown of the family as it has been known from the beginning. We said, "Anything goes." We threw away biblical values, declared God was dead, and got on with building our idols of self-help and self-esteem.

My generation was wrong—dead wrong. Hundreds of thousands of lives have been destroyed by drugs and disease. Families have been decimated. Our world is so sexualized today that we now have young children sexually experimenting in grade school. Drugs are at the core of crime all over the world because a generation demanded its freedom.

Sexual brokenness observed

I first started listening to stories of the sexually broken as a new Christian serving in the United States Air Force in the early 1970s. There I found a myriad of sexual addictions among young single men. When a roommate confessed homosexual tendencies, or the guy down the hall could not stop visiting the prostitutes downtown on a weekly basis, it put me on a quest to discover what God and His Word had to offer me and others.

I began to notice some similarities in many of their histories. I heard gut-wrenching confessions of self-hatred and emotional torment. What posed a particular issue for me was that some of these men claimed to be believers in Christ. Did I assume that as believers we were fundamentally immune to this type of behavior?

In the early '70s, there were few materials available on how to help persons wanting to recover from sexual brokenness. At the time, the only thing I knew to do was to befriend them, listen and pray with them. We would also take time to read and study the Bible together. I knew I didn't have the answers, but I had great faith that God did; we would sometimes stumble upon answers that He would reveal.

Together we frequented different churches and would hang out with friends on weekends. I discovered that the less idle time these persons had, the more they walked in freedom. I also discovered that being left alone with thoughts of depression made them vulnerable and more likely to ease that hurt with a sexual pain reliever or some other form of medication.

Drug and alcohol use and abuse were rampant on our military base. I could not help but connect the dots: taking drugs helped to reinforce how badly they felt about themselves and lowered their inhibitions. Initially, drugs and alcohol served as a numbing agent, but eventually led to guilt and remorse. I observed such self-destructive behaviors week after week. By these life patterns, they actually reinforced the very thing they were fighting: insecurity and the loss of identity.

Spiritual beings

While sexuality is tied into who we are as human beings, it is not our identity. We are not primarily sexual beings; we are primarily spiritual beings who live in a body, have a mind, will and emotions and have the capacity to act sexually. Our sexuality does not define us; God defines us as created in His image. Our spirit is the eternal part of us. It is our spirit that leads the emotional, the physical and the sexual.

When we link our identity to our sexuality, we are allowing our sexuality to define who and what we are. For example, I have never walked up to anyone and said, "Hi, my name is Steve and I am heterosexual." My heterosexuality does not define me or who I am.

I love this thought from Scripture: "For we are his workmanship created in Christ Jesus to do good works" (Ephesians 2:10). You are a product of God, not your history, not your environment and certainly not whatever lies you have been told about your sexuality and your identity. We will look at this more deeply in chapter eleven.

True freedom

It is possible to be truly free from any sin or sickness that human beings face.

What is your response to that statement? You might want to read it a second time. To be free means to live outside of bondage or slavery to sin. It means that certain sins no longer hold us captive. It means that we experience the liberty of Christ's forgiveness and let go of what enslaved us. It is defined in this verse, "It is for freedom that Christ has set us free. Stand firm, then, and do not let yourselves be burdened again by a yoke of slavery" (Galatians 5:1).

The old makes way for the new

While the Old Testament exposes the sin, the New Testament provides the truth of the Incarnate One, the Redeemer of this sin. The Old Testament scriptures are vital to understanding the new covenant. It is the old that makes a way for the new.

Far too many Christians believe that there is no need to read the books of the law or the prophets. "That was the Old Covenant," they repeat, "and we are under a new covenant." But this statement is only partially true. Jesus Himself walked on this earth under the Old Covenant, and He addressed the need for the Law of Moses.

Romans 7:7 tells us, "What shall we say then? Is the law sin? Certainly not. Indeed I would not have known what sin was except through the law." Romans 3:20 reveals that through the law we become conscious of our sin. Galatians 3:24 states, "So the law was put in charge to lead us to Christ that we might be justified by faith." And I Timothy 1:8-10 reads, "We know that the law is good if one uses it properly. We also know that law is made not for the righteous but for the lawbreakers and rebels, the ungodly and sinful, the unholy and irreligious…for those who kill…for adulterers and perverts, for slave traders…and for whatever else is contrary to the sound doctrine."

Jesus and the law

Jesus did not erase the law; rather, He fulfilled it. Remember, He lived under the Old Covenant. "Do not think that I have come to abolish the Law or the Prophets; I have not come to abolish them but to fulfill them. I tell you the truth, until heaven and earth disappear, not the smallest letter, not the least stroke of a pen, will by any means disappear from the Law until everything is accomplished. Anyone who breaks one of the least of these commandments and teaches others to do the same will be called least in the kingdom of heaven, but whoever practices and teaches these commands will be called great in the kingdom of heaven. For I tell you that unless your righteousness surpasses that of the

Pharisees and the teachers of the Law, you will certainly not enter the kingdom of heaven" (Matthew 5:17-20).

The law of the Old Covenant teaches us about sin. The Ten Commandments were given to identify sin in our lives and in society. While the law did not lead us to salvation, it made us aware of our wrongdoing. The law was good in that it showed us our sin and identified our need of a Savior. Without the law and the writings of the Old Covenant, how would we know what is offensive to our heavenly Father?

An expert in the law once asked Jesus the question, "What must I do to inherit eternal life?" Jesus responded by asking him, "What is written in the Law? How do you read it?" The man said that one was to love God with all his heart and love one's neighbor as oneself. Jesus then told him, "You have answered correctly.... Do this and you will live" (Luke 10:25-28). Was Jesus affirming the teaching of the law? Yes, He was, not as a means of gaining God's approval or love, but as a means of identifying our sinfulness.

We are discussing a vital point: the sins of the Old Testament are still sins today. While the Old Testament discussed many Jewish traditions, for our discussion we are looking at the Ten Commandments rather than the intricacies of rituals regarding dress, food or ceremonial washings. Is murder still wrong? Is stealing still wrong? Is adultery still wrong? We can still go to jail for most of these sins in our society. We must identify and accept our sinfulness in order to be healed from it.

Our justification does not come through the law; it comes through Christ (Romans 5:1). The law cannot save us; it is by faith and through grace that we are saved (Ephesians 2:5, 8). However, we must also understand that "where there is no law there is no transgression" (Romans 4:15).

No law; no transgression

When the teachers of the law brought the woman who was caught in adultery, they wanted to know (as a test) what Jesus would do with her. Both they and Jesus were aware that adultery was a sin that required death according to the law. Jesus responded that whichever one of them was without sin could cast the first stone. As they walked away one by one, He turned to the woman and forgave her. But He did more than forgive her; He told her, "Go now and leave your life of sin" (John 8:7-11). Jesus was saying that adultery is still sin, but that He had the power to forgive the sin and cleanse the sinner.

For too many, Jesus has become convenient, no more than a means to escape eternal punishment. Meanwhile, they believe they can live according to their personal interpretation of Scriptures. Jesus was a reformer, a revolutionary who taught an inconvenient reality. Even in our culture today, if you or I believe what He taught, it will be inconvenient. In fact, Jesus warned us that just as He was persecuted for what He exposed and taught, we would be as well. (See John 15:18, 19.) Further, He said that if we stand with Him and live a life honoring to Him, without compromise, there will be those who think that they do God a service by killing us. (See John 16:1-4.)

Sodom and Gomorrah

An overwhelming number of scriptures address sexual sin. Let's start with Genesis 19. Here we find the story of Sodom and Gomorrah where we discover that it did not take long for sexual brokenness to enter the world after Genesis 3. (Genesis 3 records the "fall" of man in the disobedience of His command to not eat of the tree of the knowledge of good and evil.) Two angels were visiting the city of Sodom.

Lot had them to his home for a meal and rest. Before they had retired for the evening, the men of Sodom, both young and old, were at Lot's door asking for the two visitors to come outside so that they could have sex with them (Genesis 19:5). The angels were on assignment to destroy Sodom and to get Lot and his family safely out of the city.

What would move the heart of God to the point of destroying a city? Genesis 13:13 says that the men of Sodom were "wicked" and "sinned greatly against the Lord." Even though Abraham pled for Sodom, God told him, "The outcry against Sodom and their sin is so grievous that I will go down and see if what they have done is as bad as the outcry that has reached me" (Genesis 18:20, 21).

The destruction of Sodom and Gomorrah was so complete that Jeremiah said, "God overthrew Sodom and Gomorrah along with their neighboring towns" (Genesis 50:40). The destruction of these towns is repeatedly referred to in Scripture as an example of what happens to those who engage in sexual sin. (See Jude 7 and II Peter 2:4-6.) Notably, this is where the term "sodomy" originates.

God's moral code

The Greek word *porneia* is a biblical term that means "illicit sexual intercourse," including adultery, fornication, homosexuality, bestiality and incest. Jesus used this term in Mark 10:11 when He said, "Anyone who divorces his wife and marries another woman commits *adultery* against her." The Greek term used by Jesus here was the word *porneia*. As you can see from the definition, the word had multiple sexual connotations and meanings. We should also note that the separate Greek word for just the act of adultery, *moicheia*, was not used. This is important because Jesus' words include a broader range of offenses, not just adultery.

Throughout the Old Testament, a sodomite was one who initiated licentious wickedness, the wickedness that was found within Sodom and Gomorrah. In particular, a sodomite was a person guilty of unnatural sexual relations. Leviticus 18 thoroughly discusses unlawful and unnatural sexual relations. God was so explicit because when man is left to decide for himself, he decides what is right in his own eyes, regardless of whether it is good for him or good for society as a whole. (See Psalm 36:2 and Proverbs 14:12.) God left no questions with His written moral code.

Biblical boundaries

The Scriptures forbid sex with close relatives, including one's mother, father's wife, sibling, daughter- or son-in-law, aunt and brother- or sister-in-law. Scripture also forbids having sexual intercourse with one's neighbor's wife or animals. Finally, the Scriptures say that a man is not to have sex with another man "as one lies with a woman" (Leviticus 18:6-22). God ends this chapter with a stern warning: "Everyone who does any of these detestable things—such persons must be cut off from their people. Keep my requirements and do not follow any of the detestable customs that were practiced before you came and do not defile yourselves with them. I am the Lord your God" (Leviticus 18:29, 30).

Leviticus 20 again discusses the punishment for such sin and reinforces that we need to consecrate ourselves to be holy because God is holy. This includes the statement, "If a man lies with a man as one lies with a woman, both of them have done what is detestable" (Leviticus 20:13).

As these biblical boundaries are broken in same-sex relations, "they have average life expectancy reduced by 20 years, make up more than half of the population of those diagnosed with HIV, and are much more likely to experience emotional turmoil, cases of anxiety disorders, substance abuse, depression, and suicide attempts."[1]

Jesus goes beyond the law

The Law of Moses was certainly strict. However, in Matthew 5, Jesus takes a number of issues beyond the Old Testament law. He reminded His listeners that the law said to not murder, but then added, "Anyone who is angry with his brother will be subject to judgment" (Matthew 5:22). He also affirmed that the law prohibits adultery, then adds, "But I tell you that anyone who looks at a woman lustfully has already committed adultery with her in his heart" (Matthew 5:28). Under the law, death was the requisite punishment for the act of adultery. Under grace, Jesus presents an even higher standard of purity by stating that we can commit adultery in our heart, which is just as unlawful as the act itself.

Jesus goes on to teach if one's eye is a problem (a cause of lust for sexual sin), he should remove it. He says it is better to lose a part of our body than for our whole body to be thrown into hell (Matthew 5:29). While Jesus is not recommending that we literally gouge out an eye, He is emphasizing the seriousness of sexual sin even beyond that of the requirement of the law. Jesus' teaching requires a higher standard of morality than was required in the Old Covenant.

Those we love

When a person struggling with sexual brokenness is someone we love such as a best friend, son, daughter or respected coworker, we may lose sight of these relevant biblical principles.

We should remember that God's Word never condemns the person. It condemns the sin, but also provides redemption for the sin. Jesus took the punishment we deserved and died for us on the cross. The Father placed my sin and your sin upon His Son (See Romans 5:18, 19; I Corinthians 10:13.)

Current terminology

The term "sexual brokenness" is not found in the Bible. Neither are our modern-day terms of "sexual orientation," "homosexual lifestyle," or "sexual addiction."

In *Baker's Dictionary of Biblical Terms*,[2] Bible scholar Thomas E. Schmidt writes about "the ancient world" and sexuality. He focuses on the Greco-Roman period because "there are writings from this period that demonstrate familiarity with sexual acts between members of the same gender." He states that these acts were not understood as a result of orientation, but: "It appears that the rape of the other males and the use of boys for sexual pleasure (pederasty) were performed as acts of dominance, violence, or experimentation by otherwise heterosexual men." He also states that "in some circles, most notably those of the intellectual elite philosophers and poets, relationships between men and boys were lauded as the highest expression of romantic love. These relationships were not reciprocal, however." Schmidt states that afterward, the willing or unwilling partners became "social outcasts," and some became slaves and were "discarded."[2]

In the beginning

From the beginning, God created two genders to bear His image: male and female. The Bible states that Eve was created from Adam and the two became one flesh. Adam noticed that Eve was unlike the animal kingdom when he observed that she was flesh of his flesh and bone of his bone (Genesis 2:21-25). The sexual differentiation found in Genesis 1:27 brought about the becoming of a "one flesh" union (Genesis 2:24).

The New Testament concurs with the account found in Genesis. Ephesians 5:25-31 is read at many weddings today because it gives this same scriptural order for marriage found in Genesis: "Husbands, love your wives, as Christ loved the church.... He who loves his wife loves himself.... For this reason a man will leave his father and mother and be united to his wife, and the two will become one flesh." In both the Old and New Testament, the only scriptural example of marriage given is between a man and a woman.

Paul, in the book of Romans, uses the terms "natural" and "unnatural." More specifically, he relates that women exchanged natural relations for unnatural relations and that men abandoned natural relations with women and committed indecent acts with men (Romans 1:27). What was the result? "Therefore God gave them over in the sinful desires of their hearts to sexual impurity for the degrading of their bodies with one another. They exchanged the truth of God for a lie" (Romans 1:24, 25).

This behavior was not only condemned as "deserving death," but also stated in this passage is that those who "approve of those who practice" these acts do not know God's righteousness (Romans 1:32).

Professor Rosaria Champagne Butterfield, author of the book *The Secret Thoughts of an Unlikely Convert: An English Professor's Journey into Christian Faith* wrote in a blog post on DesiringGod.org on March 2020, "I was 35 years old, called myself a lesbian, and worked as an activist and English professor in New York when I first encountered these words from Romans 1.... *Huh*, I muttered. Seems like dangerous hate speech or some other devastation designed to ruin my life. God's Word brought me to a line in the sand and a hole in my heart.

"After many years and much struggling, God used the words of Romans 1 as he led me to repentance and faith.... As I am typing these words today, having now walked with my Lord and Savior for 21 years, Romans 1 continues to impact my life."

The normal versus the abnormal

If we cannot define normal, we will not be able to define abnormal. The enemy of our soul works feverishly to make that which is normal become abnormal and that which is abnormal become normal. At one time in our nation, it would have been abnormal to become divorced from your marriage partner. Today it seems rather normal. No one seems to think twice about it. When my wife and I share that we have been married for over forty-five years, most people listening raise their eyebrows as if to say, "Wow, that's unusual," and then they congratulate us.

Abortion, at one time, would have been an anathema in the United States. Now, almost three thousand babies are murdered daily.[3] While it is abnormal behavior and the consequence of our sinful choices, it is so frequent and accepted that it has become normal to us. The enemy knows that what was once considered abnormal can be considered normal and acceptable when sin is repeated often enough.

I have watched the *Diagnostic and Statistical Manual of Mental Disorders* change several times when it comes to sexual brokenness. Psychiatrists and psychologists use this manual to diagnose disorders in order to complete treatment and administer a cure. Without a diagnosis, there is no treatment. My observation is that if the professionals cannot successfully treat and cure something labeled to be a disorder or an aberration, they then work toward the normalization of it. The treatment process then becomes attempts to help the patient normalize their behavior in his or her own mind.

Paul the Apostle was clear that those who do wrong will not inherit the kingdom of God. According to I Corinthians 6:9, "wrongdoers" include "the sexually immoral nor idolaters nor adulterers nor men who have sex with men nor thieves nor the greedy nor drunkards nor slanderers nor swindlers." Colossians reveals that we are to "put to death" that which belongs to our "earthly nature." How was that earthly nature defined? The list includes the sexually immoral, the impure, lustful evil desires and greed, which is idolatry. (See Colossians 3:5, 6.)

The good news is found in Colossians 3:7 where it says, "You used to walk in these ways, in the life you once lived." I appreciate the past tense of this verse in I Corinthians as well: "And that is what some of you were. But you were washed, you were sanctified, you were justified in the name of the Lord Jesus Christ and by the Spirit of our God" (I Corinthians 6:11). We cannot condemn those suffering from addictions. The good news is that God's love and desire is to "wash" the one struggling. There is always hope for change.

God has not wavered

The Word of God is clear about what constitutes God's gift of sex within His boundaries of love and what is outside His boundaries, noted as sinful sex.

Recorded in Acts 15 is the decision that centered on non-Jewish believers and what, if anything, would be required of them from the customs of the Jewish law. The guidelines the early church came up with for the new believers were these: "Instead we should write to them, telling them to abstain from food polluted by idols, from sexual immorality, from the meat of strangled animals and from blood" (Acts 15:20). The Greek used for "sexual immorality" was the word *porneia.* Of the regulations of the law for these new Gentile believers, it was all narrowed down to four important areas, one of those being fornication.

Sex is a generous gift from God to His creation. Unlike the animal kingdom, humans engage in sex outside of pro-creation. God designed it this way for our pleasure. When God gave us boundaries for sexuality, He also did this for our pleasure. Sexual brokenness and sexually transmitted diseases are the ongoing consequences of the crossing of these boundaries.

A better way

God has a better plan. He has always said "yes" to sex because He is the creator of it. He gives clear boundaries with that "yes" because He has our best interests in mind. We do not have the right to rewrite or change His word ac-cording to our feelings.

Sexual brokenness is a worldwide epidemic, with human sex trafficking as the newest form of slavery to plague our world. How much more wicked can our world become than to take fellow human beings, sell them into the sex trade, and then discard them as though they were worthless? The heart of God surely must be broken over such depravity.

How can we make any activity illegal or abhorrent, a "crossing over the line" if we do not uphold a standard that establishes that line to begin with? That standard must come from outside of our personal desires and emotions; otherwise it becomes what is right for me and too bad for you.

Jesus spoke these startling words of warning to His dis-ciples and to you and me: "Just as it was in the days of Noah, so also will it be in the days of the Son of Man. People were eating, drinking, marrying and being given in marriage up to the day Noah entered the ark. Then the flood came and destroyed them all. It was the same in the days of Lot. People were eating and drinking, buying and selling, planting and building. But the day Lot left Sodom, fire and sulfur rained down from heaven and destroyed them all. It will be just like this on the day the Son of Man is revealed" (Luke 17:26-30).

Will you be ready for the day Jesus is speaking about? I believe God is looking on the earth once again to find the righteous ones like Lot and Noah who live in purity and obedience to God and will speak His truth as His representatives. We cannot force people to repent for their sin and change their ways, but it is our job to tell them the good news of Christ while doing good works in love and compassion.

Things have changed

Since I was younger and in the military, the world around me has changed concerning sexual brokenness. We can consider just the area of same-sex attraction.

When I first learned of this among my friends it was simply something that some people irregularly practiced or experimented with. Then it became a condition, a sexual confusion in which there needed to be change through professional intervention. In time it became politicized and was eventually called a "sexual orientation." Today we can see or observe it as a longing for personal identity. Many no longer call themselves homosexual, but gay, attaching themselves to a community of people who identify themselves in this way. In many Western nations, new laws reinforce these changes.

In 2015 the United States Supreme Court decided to legalize gay marriage. Author Rosaria Butterfield writes insightfully, "Obergefell ushered in a new world, one where the fragmented LGBTQ community on the margins became the united LGBTQ machine calling the shots from the center. Three things resulted: (1) Obergefell codified the idea that sexual orientation is a category of personhood; in reality, sexual orientation is a category mistake that comes from Sigmund Freud. (2) Obergefell expanded civil rights to include protecting the dignity of someone who identifies as LGBTQ; the vague and subjective nature of this legal language has contributed to a world where hurt feelings reign supreme. (3) Obergefell put religious liberty on the firing line, as it pitted the teaching of the Bible against the teaching of the Supreme Court. After Obergefell, LGBTQ is now 'who' you are, not only 'how' you feel."[4]

Pornography feeds the storm

To add to the tragedy of our day, we have something called pornography. At one time it was difficult to obtain as one had to visit seedy places to purchase it. Today, all we need to do is turn on our phone or computer and, *voilà*, we can find any form of destructive, degrading, demeaning and devaluing film that we desire to view. The incidents of pornography use are starting with children in grade school. Pornography is highly addictive. It has destroyed individual lives and shattered whole families.

The viewing of pornography feeds an industry of sex trafficking, disease and death. Mind, soul and spirit are polluted. Pornography takes the sexual gift God gave to us and perverts it for short-term gratification and lust-filled pleasure.

If you are viewing pornography, you are tearing down any sense of esteem and identity that God is desiring to build within you. There is nothing redemptive about this sin-filled habit. I appeal to you to seek immediate help.

Pressing toward a new goal

Not that I have already obtained all this, or have already arrived at my goal, but I press on to take hold of that for which

Christ Jesus took hold of me. Brothers and sisters, I do not consider myself yet to have taken hold of it. But one thing I do: Forgetting what is behind and straining toward what is ahead, I press on toward the goal to win the prize for which God has called me heavenward in Christ Jesus. All of us, then, who are mature should take such a view of things. And if on some point you think differently, that too God will make clear to you. Only let us live up to what we have already attained. Join together in following my example, brothers and sisters, and just as you have us as a model, keep your eyes on those who live as we do. For, as I have often told you before and now tell you again even with tears, many live as enemies of the cross of Christ. Their destiny is destruction, their god is their stomach, and their glory is in their shame. Their mind is set on earthly things. But our citizenship is in heaven. And we eagerly await a Savior from there, the Lord Jesus Christ, who, by the power that enables him to bring everything under his control, will transform our lowly bodies so that they will be like his glorious body" (Philippians 3:12-21).

Paul the Apostle at one time zealously persecuted Christians, but had a dramatic encounter with the living God. In the words above, he encourages us to press on toward the goal for which Christ took hold of us, to forget what is behind, and to look ahead. In all we think, in all we speak, and in all we do, our goal is to be like our Lord and Savior. He gave His life so that we can walk in sexual freedom in obedience to Him.

Let us live knowing that our bodies are temporary, our spirits are eternal, and that Christ has made a way for us to live with Him eternally.

In the next chapter, we will consider more carefully how our sexual orientation does not determine our identity or our future eternity.

REFLECT AND DISCUSS

1. How have you observed sexual brokenness in your life and the lives of those around you?

2. What are your thoughts about Jesus and the law and how He addressed it during His time on the earth?

3. Are there things that were, in your own lifetime, abnormal but are becoming normalized?

4. How would you share with someone that God's boundaries concerning sex are worth obeying?

Suggested books, videos and support group resources

Healing the Wounds of Sexual Addiction by Dr. Mark Laaser

Shattered Vows: Hope and Healing for Women Who Have Been Sexually Betrayed by Debra Laaser

The Conquer Series DVD from KingdomWorks Studios

www.celebraterecovery.com – a Christian 12-step recovery program

www.puredesire.org – a safe place for recovery from pornography addiction and unwanted sexual behavior

www.fightthenewdrug.org – a website dedicated to stopping human trafficking and pornography

ENDNOTES

1. Ken Williams, "Wholeness and Freedom from Sexual Brokeness," Destiny Image, accessed March 22, 2021, https://www.destinyimage.com/blog/ken-williams-wholeness-and-freedom-from-sexual-brokenness.

2. Thomas E. Schmidt, *Baker's Dictionary of Biblical Terms*, www.biblestudytools.com.

3. www.worldometers.info/abortions.

4. Rosaria Butterfield, "Are We Living out Romans 1?", *Desiring God*, February 27, 2020, https://www.desiringgod.org/articles/are-we-living-out-romans-1.

I am free from all condemnation.

Romans 8:1

I am kept from falling
and presented without fault.

Jude 24

I am accepted by Christ.

Romans 15:7

I have died to sin...
but am alive to God.

Romans 6:2, 11

We fix our eyes on the things that
cannot be seen, because
they will last forever.

II Corinthians 4:18

CHAPTER ELEVEN

Sex and Gender ID

When people get married because they think it's a long-time love affair, they'll be divorced very soon, because all love affairs end in disappointment. But marriage is a recognition of a spiritual identity. — Joseph Campbell

If I had to label myself, I would label myself as a gay man. With that said, I believe that love is the only thing that matters, and I would hope that anybody would leave themselves open—not to gender, but to love....
If I fall in love down the road with a woman, I'm going to love that woman. — Jussie Smollett

A gender-equal society would be one where the word gender *does not exist: where everyone can be themselves.* — Gloria Steinem

One may think the cure for multiple forms of sexual dysphoria or brokenness is a heterosexual orientation. To me, this is far from adequate. If sexual orientation is our goal, but we do not transform our thought processes, hearts and eventually identity, we are no different than an alcoholic whose only goal is to quit drinking. Yes, that is a huge step in the right direction, but it is only the tip of the iceberg in the process of life change. The orientation for or against alcohol does not change the heart.

Reaching out to the homeless

Our family and small group have opportunity to reach

out to and care for the homeless in Philadelphia, Pennsylvania, through a friend's ministry. On occasion, we run into the nontypical homeless person who tells us, "I really do not need your help. I know where I can sleep and eat every day. I know where to obtain clothing and other needed items because I choose to be homeless. Homelessness is what I do." Based on these experiences, I would be incorrect to say that every homeless person wants to make changes in life so they will no longer be homeless.

While it may seem foreign to many of us, we have found that some people choose homelessness. It is what they know and what they desire for their lives. In a similar way, some individuals choose a specific sexual orientation because it is what they know or the way they have been thinking for as long as they can remember.

It would seem reasonable then, if we are created as male and female for the purpose of reflecting the image of God, that Satan desires to warp, or even destroy, this belief. In an attempt to convince mankind there is no distinct male or female orientation, our identity as being created in God's image can take on many different feelings and reactions or be denied altogether.

Quotes

The quotations at the beginning of this chapter identify the confusion people feel about sexuality or gender. In response to Gloria Steinem's quote, we might ask, "Would the nonexistence of the word *gender* in our society really give more opportunity for everyone to 'be themselves'?" What does that even mean?

In a current dictionary, *gender* is defined as "either the male or female decision of a species, especially as differentiated by social and cultural roles and behavior" (dictionary.

com). In the *World Book Encyclopedia Dictionary* from 1967 the definition of *gender* is simply given as, "sex." Do you notice the difference? One has evolved to a "decision…as differentiated by social and cultural roles and behavior." The other simply related gender to one's sex: male or female.

We were created for something different

You and I were created by God to live in a Genesis one and two world. What does that mean? Genesis chapters one and two are the only chapters in the Bible that describe what life was like before "the curse" became the course of each and every life born thereafter.

In these first two chapters of Genesis the Bible describes God's relationship with man as literally meeting with him, walking with him and conversing with him on a daily basis. Every day, God's presence would meet with Adam and God would instruct him about the garden. In those conversations God would personally feel Adam's loneliness on the earth. God would soon "fashion" a woman, flesh of Adam's flesh and bone of his bone. It was here, in this garden, that God created something we call marriage: "For this reason a man will leave his father and mother and be united to his wife, and the two will become one flesh" (Genesis 2:24). Marriage was and is a creation act of God, not an act of man.

At the same time, the seas were teeming with fish and the air with birds. God said that the land was to produce all kinds of livestock and wild animals. There was an endless variety of plant life and God placed Adam in a garden to care for it and to watch it multiply. There were no weeds, no bugs, no diseases and no harmful or dangerous conditions. The world and everything in it was perfect.

Then comes Genesis 3, the chapter which describes "the fall of man." It is here that deception, fear, disease, insecurity, disobedience and the loss of our God-given identity entered the world. Life on this earth would be forever changed by hearts that wanted something more than they already had in the garden. Adam and Eve longed for a knowledge that was not theirs to have. God was trying to protect us from ourselves, but also in His wisdom, He gave us free choice.

God created us and blessed us to live in a Genesis one and two world, but we chose a fallen world, a world of disobedience, death and missing the mark of God's ideal for His creation. Ever since this time we have been left to pursue what we think is right in our own eyes. (See Proverbs 12:15; 21:2.) The Genesis 3 account makes a huge statement about the deceitfulness of the heart of man. The heart of mankind cannot always be trusted to reveal truth to our thoughts, feelings and actions.

"A good man brings good things out of the good stored up in his heart, and an evil man brings evil things out of the evil stored up in his heart. For the mouth speaks what the heart is full of" (Luke 6:45).

Learning from science

The American Psychological Association has written, "There is no consensus among scientists about the exact reasons that an individual develops a heterosexual, bisexual, gay or lesbian orientation. Although much research has examined the possible genetic, hormonal, developmental, social, and cultural influences on sexual orientation, no findings have emerged that permit scientists to conclude that sexual orientation is determined by any particular factor or factors."[1]

In 2016, scholars at Johns Hopkins University in Maryland released a 143-page report that argues there is not enough definitive scientific evidence available to suggest that gay, lesbian and transgender individuals are born with a certain sexual orientation or gender identity. [2]

In the three-part report, Lawrence Mayer, a scholar-in-residence at Johns Hopkins University's psychiatry department and a professor of statistics and biostatistics at Arizona State University, and Paul McHugh, a professor of psychiatry and behavioral sciences at Johns Hopkins, take on prevailing claims that sexual orientation and gender dysphoria are caused by natural traits. The scholars challenge the claim that discrimination and social stigma is the sole reason why those with same-sex attractions or transgender identity suffer higher rates of mental health problems.

The report argues there is insufficient evidence to claim that heterosexual, homosexual or bisexual attractions are an innate trait that people are born with. It also looks at other evidence of hypothesized biological causes, such as prenatal development and hormones but finds that evidence is also limited.

"Studies of the brains of homosexuals and heterosexuals have found some differences, but have not demonstrated that these differences are inborn rather than the result of environmental factors that influenced both psychological and neurobiological traits," the report reads. "One environmental factor that appears to be correlated with non-heterosexuality is childhood sexual abuse victimization, which may also contribute to the higher rates."[3]

Some evidence suggests that sexual orientation is fluid.

A study by the National Longitudinal Study of Adolescent to Adult Health[4] tracked the sexual orientation of children aged seven to twelve years in 1994-1995 and again in 2007-2008 when they were young adults.

The study found that 80 percent of male respondents who had reported same-sex attraction and both-sex attraction in their childhood later identified as exclusively heterosexual. Meanwhile, more than half of the female respondents who reported both-sex attractions as children reported being exclusively attracted to males as adults.

Lawrence Mayer of Johns Hopkins University told the *Christian Post*, "The idea [there is] that sexual orientation is fluid, that people change as people grow. There are probably some people that identify as heterosexual that then later on identified as homosexual, so it goes both ways. The importance there is the fluidity and flexibility that these things change in time."[5]

Although some studies have found that brain activation patterns differ among people who identify as members of the opposite biological sex, the scholars hold that as follows: "These studies do not offer sufficient evidence for drawing sound conclusions about possible associations between brain activation and sexual identity or arousal. The results are conflicting and confusing.

"The question is not simply whether there are differences between the brains of transgender individuals and people identifying with the gender corresponding to their biological sex, but whether gender identity is a fixed, innate, and biological trait, even when it does not correspond to biological sex, or whether environmental or psychological causes contribute to the development of a sense of gender identity might be the consequence of biological factors such as genes or prenatal hormone exposure, or of psychological and environmental factors such as childhood abuse, or they could result from some combination of the two."[6]

Science is not my point

While the nature of this book is not primarily scientific, the point is that social scientists do not agree on these arguments. Even science, however, is being manipulated today by the feelings of those who sense a strong direction one way or another. Perhaps what scientists do agree on is that many sexual orientations exist in our world today. That has caused legislators to change the laws and allow people to self-identify concerning gender with or without surgical transition. We make a choice to act on what we feel or to not act upon what we feel.

Sex and gender identity

Andrew Walker in his excellent book titled *God and the Transgender Debate* states, "Gender has always been expressed in different ways. What has changed today is that many now see gender as unattached to sex. That is, you don't just express gender differently; you can be a different gender. Your sex may be 'female,' but that does not necessarily mean that you—as regards your gender—are 'female.'"[7]

Due to medical advances, we can now seek a gender that is different from our sex. If one's sex is male, that same person can have their body surgically adjusted so as to imitate the female gender. This has led to the term "gender identity." "Gender dysphoria" is a term used when someone is experiencing an incongruity between their gender and their biological sex or body.

For these persons, this is a real-life issue and one that can create anxiety, depression, rejection and many other real feelings. I cannot even imagine what these persons must go through on a daily basis and I cannot claim to understand. But at the same time, I do know that God and His Word have given us life designs, hope and truth. God gives us, however, complete freedom to think, feel and make decisions for ourselves. We can accept or reject God's guidelines.

But it's sin, right?

Let's take a step back and consider feelings versus actions. While I may feel like hurting you in my anger, I can choose not to act on that feeling. Anger that is out-of-control anger, or rage, is wrong, while anger as a feeling is not.

Using that principle, we can say that if I feel like I am the opposite sex and experience gender dysphoria, it is not a sin. I still have the choice to either act on or not act on that feeling. In the same way, persons with severe depression may feel and even express the desire to commit suicide. The person experiencing such a deep level of duress must make the decision not to act upon what they are feeling to avoid loss of life. The feeling in and of itself, because of the mental instability of depression, is not sin.

It is dangerous to self-approve of every feeling we experience; feelings are not necessarily true. Even if I have felt like the opposite sex for as long as I can remember, that historical feeling or the length of time I have had that feeling does not make it true.

Being involved in years of counseling has afforded me the opportunity to hear plenty of horror stories. I can still recall Lisa's story that resulted in severe anorexia. While her story and her pain were true, she was acting out self-destructive behavior, starving herself to death. If I would have merely affirmed every feeling that Lisa had, it would have been cruel. Further, if I would have commented that her self-perception of being obese was right in an effort to validate her feelings, I would have been both unprofessional and dishonest.

We all struggle with sin. (See Romans 3:23.) God's answer is the same to each of us. He longs to bring His identity to us, but that will not happen as long as we insist on living by and through our feelings. As we seek Him and give Him our lives, He will create us anew, transforming us into a new creation. The old passes away and the new comes. (See II Corinthians 5:17.)

I fully believe that if one single wrong thought or wrong-doing can be eradicated, changed and redeemed by our God, then any type of gender dysphoria can be eradicated and changed, if desired, as well.

Is there a biblical precedent about transgenderism?

We looked at scriptures related to sexuality in chapter ten. There are limited scriptures to add specific to transgenderism. Deuteronomy 22:5 discusses cross-dressing, but not transgenderism. I Corinthians 6:9 describes men having sex with men as immoral. We also have Jesus' discussion in Matthew 19:12 about the three types of eunuchs: those born this way (unable to procreate), those made this way (by castration) and those who choose a celibate lifestyle. The broader question that Jesus was answering in Matthew 19 was concerning marriage and divorce between a man and a woman.[8]

Concerning eunuchs, we have the wonderful story of Philip the evangelist and how he reached out to the Ethiopian eunuch after receiving a direct assignment from God to do so. Acts 8 reveals the story of the eunuch finding Jesus as His Savior while reading the book of Isaiah in his chariot.

It was Isaiah the prophet who described how the Lord welcomes the outsider and makes room for the marginalized, the eunuchs "who keep [God's] Sabbaths, who chose what pleases [Him] and hold fast to [His] covenant" (Isaiah 56:4).[9]

The Bible consistently recognizes two genders: male and female. These two separate yet harmonious sexes are given the gift, through marriage, of creating another human being.[10]

The identity question is a huge one for the person who sees themselves as transgender. That question of identity has now changed to, "What do I identify as?" We can maintain the best theology ever and miss the person who is struggling right in front of us. Our theology will never save anyone, but that certainly does not mean we have none or that we keep good theology to ourselves. Perhaps it's not what is said, but how lovingly we say it.

Bioethics and Christian ethicist H. Tristram Engelhardt writes, "It is not Christianity's job to blend in or make itself more palatable to secular, pluralistic society. Rather, the mystery and exclusive nature of Christianity invites others to explore and be drawn into the faith."[11]

For anyone who feels they hold to a certain truth that simultaneously goes against what society or culture is telling them, it takes certain courage to stick by that truth. The pressure to acquiesce to the popular opinion of the day could force us to compromise our convictions.

There is a saying, "Sometimes the truth hurts." That does not mean we have license to be hurtful with the truth; that would be mean-spiritedness. While Jesus spoke the truth, He did so in love and grace. We can speak truth as long as grace is our means.

The case of Chloe

My friend Chloe (not her real name) was working as a hairstylist in the 1980s to the 1990s. She shared with me that at the time she had no relationship with God. Chloe was raised by her mother with no dad in the picture. She said that based on her work, "I took on the identity of a hairstylist." I asked her what that meant. "I worked twelve hours a day doing women's hair; it's what I did and it was who I became. I took on the life of a hairstylist. I partied and I had sex," she explained.

Chloe said she had "experimented" with girlfriends in junior high school, but never believed herself to be a lesbian. One day the owner of her shop who was a gay man began the rumor that one of the hairdressers was attracted to Chloe. I asked her how that made her feel. She said, "I was intrigued with the relationship. It never went anywhere, but it sowed a seed in my life." She continued, "So I began to visit gay bars and welcomed the fact that other women were attracted to me. I had more relationships. I still did not see myself as a lesbian, but continued to believe it to be a hairstylist's identity. It provided some security to me. At the time, I was more secure with a woman than with a man."

Chloe also told me that as a child, one babysitter "had a brother and a father who repeatedly molested me." She continued, "Once on a date, I was raped. Women were safer to me. Besides, my mother always told me that I didn't need a man; I only had to take care of myself. I learned from my mother that men were not dependable. So, for ten years I had relationship after relationship with mostly women—and then I met my husband."

Her story goes on, "Our baby daughter became our glue because our marriage was a mess and almost crashed several times. During those difficult times I kept telling myself that I must be a lesbian because those were the only relationships I was attracted to and found myself continually fantasizing about."

But things were about to change for Chloe, radically change. I asked her what had made the difference in her marriage, because when I interviewed Chloe they had just celebrated their 25th anniversary. She said, "I found Jesus!"

Chloe told me that she received an unexpected call from her father after not hearing from him or seeing him since she was four years old. He invited her to a family reunion where she met her Uncle Don, a truck driver who was passionate about and "on fire" for Jesus. She said he came right up to her and said, "Hi, I'm your Uncle Don. Do you know Jesus? Do you place Him first in your life?" Chloe said she felt "hot all over" and started to stutter, not knowing what to say. "Uncle Don took me aside and then shared his story with me. He wasn't religious about his faith, just real," she said.

I asked Chloe what happened next and she said, "Well, at the time, I discovered that my husband was not being faithful to me, but I felt trapped with no job, no money and a baby. I didn't know what to do. I remember running out of the house one day to the cemetery. I pressed myself up against a large tree and began to scream at the top of my lungs. I screamed at God and I told Him that my marriage sucked. I screamed at my husband. How did God ever think that marriage was a good idea? When I was all done screaming, I heard two questions from this gentle voice: 'Do you know Jesus and do you place Him first in your life?'"

Chloe told me, "My identity had been nothing but brokenness and betrayal. However, when I received Jesus, asking Him into my heart, He became my identity." Chloe said, "My anger at my husband, my identity as a hairstylist and my broken heart were mended that day—all washed away—as I surrendered. My heart was hardened and physically hurting. I felt Jesus reach in and literally massage my heart, removing my hurt."

"I began a new love affair. I was so passionately in love with Jesus and I just knew He was real," she told me. "In fact," she said, "I just kept repeating over and over and over, You're real, You're so very real."

Chloe told me, "My new identity was fully and completely in His love for me; it was so tangible. I hungered for the Bible because in it I found I could better know Him. I learned what marriage is supposed to look like from God's Word. I was done protecting myself; I allowed God to be my Protector."

I asked Chloe's husband what he thought of the change in his wife. "I literally saw the complete transformation in my wife and within two weeks I came to Jesus myself," he said. "Our marriage is a miracle and we are more in love every day."

I then asked Chloe what she would tell someone who struggles with identity in sexuality and marriage. Chloe said, "I would tell them how valuable they are to God and how much He loves them. I would tell them He is your real Father and He wants to protect you and heal your broken heart. He is right there; just reach out to Him."

We are more than our sexual feelings

Every one of us are far more than our sexual desires, dreams or feelings. We are not defined by these things. Author Glenn Stanton writes, "Male and female, marriage and family are not so-called cultural constructs. An androgenized humanity, family, and culture are all culturally constructed and artificially forced upon a culture by ideological and political pressure. It does not follow that same-sex attraction or identity is like either ethnicity or race. No sexual attraction is."[12]

In the case of Chloe, so much of life, good and bad, fed into her decisions and beliefs about herself. So many of those beliefs came from her history. I concur with what

Jim Anderson writes in his book *Unmasked*, "God's beautiful developmental design in the formation of a daughter's identity through her father gives us great reason to value and encourage the strengthening of this father-daughter bond. God took all into consideration when He made the blueprint for the family. The identity formation begins during those important early years in a young girl's life when she is "female but not sexual." In that season, God intends for her to be filled with a sense of self-worth and value by words, non-sexual touch, and attention from her father: The three A's that must be employed by a father in his daughter's life are: Affirmation – the power of his words. Affection – the power of his touch. Attention – the power of his time and his heart's focus."[13]

Maybe you did not receive affirmation, affection or attention from your father or mother—and perhaps you never will. (We will discuss this in more depth in chapter 16.) That does not change the fact that you do have all of God's affirmation, affection and attention.

However, as was the case with Chloe, we have a huge propensity to seek worth and value in anything but God. If we find that worth and value in hairdressing or whatever our identity might be, the longer we pursue those things, the more defining they become for us. If we continually embrace a lie instead of the truth concerning our identity, we will live in a constant struggle.

Chloe saw herself as "Hairstylist Chloe" and then lived her life according to her beliefs about hairstylists. But our identity in Christ cannot be varied by any connected adjective such as:

I am a feminist Christian

I am a black Christian

I am a fundamental Christian

I am a gay Christian

I am a hairstylist Christian

I am simply and completely a follower of Christ who has received all of my identity from Christ and who He says I am. We are told in Romans 12:1, 2, "Offer your bodies as living sacrifices, holy and pleasing to God—this is your spiritual act of worship. Do not conform any longer to the pattern of this world, but be transformed by the renewing of your mind." We are being transformed from what we thought we once were to become who He says we already are.

Paul the Apostle alludes to this in Ephesians 2 where he states that when we walk in our "transgressions" and "idolatry," we walked in "darkness," "gratifying our fleshly desires." Then Paul acknowledges, "But because of his great love for us, God, who is rich in mercy, made us alive with Christ even when we were dead in our transgressions.... For we are God's handiwork" (Ephesians 2:4, 5, 10). We were pursuing darkness, but God who is so rich in love and mercy pursued us! In this reality, we are given a brand-new identity.

Denying self

In Matthew 16:24, 25, Jesus said, "If anyone would come after me, let him deny himself and take up his cross and follow me. For whoever would save his life will lose it, but whoever loses his life for my sake will find it." To carry a cross means to deny ourselves—to lose whatever defined and directed our lives before we met our Maker and accepted Him as Savior.

In pleading with God to take away an issue in his life, Paul wrote, "But he said to me, 'My grace is sufficient for you, for my power is made perfect in weakness.' Therefore I will boast all the more gladly about my weaknesses, so that

Christ's power may rest on me.... When I am weak, then I am strong" (II Corinthians 12:9, 10).

Not one of us seeks a cross to carry. We would like a carefree life, and we abhor the uncomfortable. As I travel the world, I have seen the slum where three quarters of a million people live in Kenya. I have seen the poverty and the lack of any governmental control in Haiti. I have been in places where overcontrolling governments say that Christianity cannot be openly practiced. These believers live daily with these crosses, and they take them on willingly as normality without complaint.

If you deal with gender dysphoria or sexual broken-ness, then you too have a cross to bear. But that cross is not permanent. Just like in the life of Chloe, there is life ahead, because life is from the God whom we serve. In *You Are the Beloved*, Henri Nouwen wrote, "The great spiritual call of the Beloved Children of God is to pull their brokenness away from the shadow of the curse and put it under the light of the blessing. This is not as easy as it sounds. The power of darkness around us is strong, and our world finds it easier to manipulate self-rejecting people than self-accepting people. But when we keep listening attentively to the Voice calling us the Beloved, it becomes possible to live our brokenness, not as a confirmation of our fear that we are worthless, but as an opportunity to purify and deepen the blessing that rests upon us. Physical, mental, or emotional pain lived under the blessing is experienced in ways radically different from physical, mental, or emotional pain lived under the curse."[14]

Gender dysphoria among our youth

Newsweek magazine printed an opinion article titled "We Need Balance When It Comes to Gender Dysphoric Kids.

I Would Know." The article was written by Scott Newgent, a 48-year-old transgendered man. He writes, "I was thrilled when the medical community told me six years ago that I could change from a woman to a man. I was informed about all the wonderful things that would happen due to medical transition, but all the negatives were glossed over. Since then, I have suffered tremendously, including seven surgeries, a pulmonary embolism, an induced stress heart attack, sepsis, a 17-month recurring infection, 16 rounds of antibiotics, three weeks of daily IV antibiotics, arm reconstructive surgery, lung, heart and bladder damage, insomnia, hallucinations, PTSD, $1 million in medical expenses, and loss of home, car, career and marriage. All this, and yet I cannot sue the surgeon responsible–in part because there is no structured, tested or widely accepted baseline for transgender health care."[15]

Transgender health care is experimental, yet the industry is encouraging minors to transition as well. Obviously, there are huge profits to be made, but at what expense? Scott goes on to declare that children have no ability to understand something that can take "a lifetime to understand." He states that no child is capable of consenting to "decreased life expectancy, bone damage, possible liver damage, increased mental health complications, higher suicide rates than non-trans population, twelve percent higher chance than non-trans population to develop symptoms of psychosis, chances of stunted brain development, much reduced chance for lifelong sexual pleasure, higher chance of sterility and infertility, no improved mental health outcomes and not [being] completely reversible."[16]

There have been no long-term studies to determine the ramifications and psychological effects of transitioning on children. Often, the parties who bravely raise the questions are quickly shut down.

Scott further relates that America is headed down a path of affirmation while many European countries are now "restoring greater balance...overhauling [their] approach to treating minors with gender dysphoria, prioritizing psychotherapeutic non-invasive interventions and recognizing adolescence as a time of major identity exploration."[17]

Pursuing a sexual identity for all the wrong reasons

When our sexuality becomes who we are or how we express our identity, we will be disappointed. It is an expectation that sexuality cannot deliver because our sexuality is only a part of our whole being.

To pursue an identity in our sexuality for the purpose of obtaining self-esteem will ultimately disappoint. Having the attention of someone sexually may empower for a moment, but that moment will end quickly. We will have to keep chasing that feeling through multiple relationships. In time, one's sense of self will be destroyed due to losing oneself and one's personal worth in multiple relationships.

There are also those who through life circumstances have taken on hurts due to the real or perceived control of others in their life. Such persons might look for identity in their sexuality in order to feel powerful or in control. This is when sex becomes a weapon utilized to control another, an expression of power, so to speak.

It is also detrimental to look for our identity in the sexual realm because it is the popular thing to do. Many junior and senior high age youth are pursuing sexuality in this way in order to feel popular. When we choose the popularity message rather than the courageous one, we will find ourselves compromising our identity.

There are also those who seek out sexuality as an identity because they feel lost and alone. Out of aloneness they pursue sexuality in order to feel needed or wanted. This can set off a life pattern of pursuing sexuality with almost anyone and can end in even more insecurity and loss of personal identity.

In all of these examples, we are missing the whole point of God's created act of sex. Never has God in His Word connected our sexuality to our esteem, our need for relationship, our popularity or our desire to overcome aloneness. All of these expressions are far less than the reasons for His creative act of sex. God's expression of sexuality has always been to love and be loved within His boundaries.

We are not to be like the Pharisees

Jesus was drawn toward those who, as He said, needed a doctor, not those who superficially thought they were okay. (See Mark 2:17.) Taking a moment to lay aside the subject of sexual brokenness or gender identity, we could first talk about the heart of man. When the heart is ministered to and becomes right before God, all life issues can be addressed by God in His way and in His time. How did Jesus see you when you were living without Him? Was your sin (literally, missing the mark) any different than my sin? Jesus noticed and was drawn to Zacchaeus in the tree, the woman at the well, the blind beggar and the woman caught in adultery. He didn't just see them; He saw through them, straight into their hearts.

One day when Jesus was at a Pharisee's home for dinner, a "questionable" woman with an alabaster jar of perfume showed up. She began to soak Jesus' feet with her tears of repentance and pour oil on Him. The Pharisee said, "If this man were a prophet, he would know who is touching him and what kind of woman she is—that she is a sinner." Jesus responds with a parable, then firmly states, "'Therefore, I tell you, her many sins have been forgiven—as her great love has shown. But whoever has been forgiven little loves little.' Then Jesus said to her, 'Your sins are forgiven'" (Luke 7:36-48).

Jesus saw deep repentance in the tears of this woman because He could see into her heart. He knew that this level of genuineness and authenticity was not just contrition. It was deep and truth-filled sorrow over her lifestyle and her past. She found her Savior, then fell on her knees before Him to wash His feet.

The church is not to be like the Pharisee who looked down on this woman, but like Jesus who received her. Luke 18 gives an interesting description of the pride-filled Christian who looks down on the one who struggles with life-controlling sin. It says, "To some who were confident of their own righteousness and looked down on everyone else, Jesus told this parable" (Luke 18:9). That parable was about two very different men who approached God in two very different ways: a tax collector and a Pharisee. One was repentant and one was filled with self-pride. The latter was expressing how much "less" of a sinner he was than the tax collector.

People who struggle with drugs, sexual issues or depression can quickly see through the pride-filled believer who presumes to be better than others. They quickly read the rejection and the law-filled judgment. They have a keen sense of who is genuine and authentic and who is superficial. Pharisaical judgments will never change a heart or a life.

We could be committing sins of gossip, overeating, jealousy, critical judgments, hatred, comparison or pride and think that somehow those sins are benign. They are not. We all need the cross and we all need deep repentance in our life because we all need forgiveness.

What are you waiting for?

My son returned home from his second year of college and with a look of confusion and compassion asked me, "Dad, what about those persons who are attracted to the same sex only? They are not attracted to the opposite sex. They are the butt of jokes. I hear their stories and I am hurting for them. Where do they stand? What about love for them?" It was one of the most difficult questions I was asked while raising children, and I knew it to be a defining moment.

Every day we each make a choice to act on our thoughts and feelings or not to act upon them. Every day we make a choice to honor and obey what we understand to be the truth in God's Word or cast it off as obsolete and old-fashioned. Maybe you have never struggled in any area of sexuality, but you have a choice to make as well.

You do not have to be same-sex attracted to have a choice. Those who are heterosexual and have always been heterosexual have a choice, too. Every day we choose to either obey God in our sexuality or to not obey Him. It can be a temptation as great as being unfaithful to our vows and thereby hurting everyone around us. It could be a temptation to view pornography. Certainly, pornography for the heterosexual is as wrong as pornography for the homosexual or transgendered person.

We each have a choice to make. We choose to submit our sexuality to God and His plan, or we choose not to. Either God's grace is sufficient, no matter what we deal with, or we determine it is not. Either way, we are left with the consequences of our decisions. Deciding God's way may mean having a certain cross to bear, but it will lead us into an eternity of God's pleasure. He is preparing a place for us and longs for each of us to make choices that will usher us into that place. (See John 14:1-3.)

When we make a declaration that it is God's way and God's way only, will He not make a way of escape? Will He not come alongside you, strengthen you and lift you up? Will He not understand the temptation that you go through and with that temptation provide a way through the temptation to victory? (See I Corinthians 10:13.)

Every one of us is in a battle; it's a battle that began in Genesis 3. We have been lied to, stolen from, and harassed. The evil one has even attempted to rob us of our very lives, but God has come to give us our lives back. (See John 10:10.) We each walk in brokenness. Will we choose God's way and allow that brokenness to turn into a story of redemption? We can make the choice to live within God's divine destiny for our lives.

"Be alert and of sober mind. Your enemy the devil prowls around like a roaring lion looking for someone to devour. Resist him, standing firm in the faith, because you know that the family of believers throughout the world is undergoing the same kind of sufferings.

"And the God of all grace, who called you to his eternal glory in Christ, after you have suffered a little while, will himself restore you and make you strong, firm and steadfast. To him be the power for ever and ever. Amen" (I Peter 5:8-11).

Closing reflections toward healing

1. Not every life challenge will be removed from us on this earth. But I know, without a single doubt, the God who loved me and gave Himself for me has never left me nor forsaken me. He is with me and is bringing me into His destiny planned from eternity past to eternity future. We can trust Him.

2. In a quiet moment before God, ask Him to speak to you about yourself. What and how does He personally desire to speak to you, to affirm you, to correct and to love you? Express your feelings concerning your sexual choices and ask Him to share His heart with you through His Word and His Spirit. Confess to Him and receive His forgiveness. The Lord is not ashamed of you. From the cross He says, "Shame off of you" as He removes the burden of your sin and guilt.

3. Have you felt pressured by others to conform to an image which you are not convinced is the real you? Allow God to call your name and speak to you about how He sees you. Allow Him to reveal the destiny He has had for you since before you were born. Have you been hurt or abused by persons who were close to you? Bring your pain, your brokenness and your disappointment to Him and ask Him to help you forgive those who hurt you. Speak forgiveness to each one of those persons by name.

4. The word "authentic" has come to be understood as an expression of who I must be—authentic, true to myself as I define myself. When you are being authentic with yourself in your quiet moments, are you happy? Are you experiencing deep joy and fulfillment? Further, can you allow others to be authentic with you and bring a message that is different than the one you have been telling yourself about yourself? The authentic message in this book is to reveal to you who and whose you really are when you are in Christ.

5. The following scriptural process gives us a definition of change. "Can the Ethiopian change his skin or the leopard its spots? Neither can you do good who are accustomed to doing evil" (Jeremiah 13:23). Notice the words "accustomed to." Now we go to Proverbs 14:23 which reads, "All hard work brings a profit, but mere talk leads only to poverty." No doubt, it is "hard work" to change anything in our lives. Finally, Hebrews 5:14 states, "But solid food is for the mature, who by constant use have trained themselves to distinguish good from evil." While the language can feel strong, these verses are simply saying we can change even if we are accustomed to another way. It may be hard work, but if we only talk about change, it will not happen. As we receive the "solid food" from God which is truth, with constant use we can retrain our thoughts to become His thoughts and our feelings to be His feelings.

6. Psalm 42:5 conveys the important truth that we are never hopeless. The psalmist asked himself why his soul was feeling so "downcast" and "disturbed," but then says, "Put your hope in God, for I will yet praise him, my Savior, my God." You are never hopeless in God; you are never without a choice. Those who become hopeless or completely disturbed and feel as though they have no choice left in life are marking themselves to be victims.

7. Many resources are available for those who desire counsel and personal life change. Some references are provided at the end of this chapter. Godly input is available in books and videos from loving and caring voices, many of whom have themselves struggled with or presently struggle with sexual brokenness.

Consider praying this prayer of confession with me

Father, thank You for so generously giving to me Your Son, Jesus. Thank You that He bore my sin, my shame and my brokenness on the cross. Thank You, Jesus, that you have forgiven me and removed all shame from me. I am cleansed; I am washed and I am free from my past so that I can walk in the purposes that You planned for me. Your dreams for me will not be stopped by my history, but rather I now walk in a brand new day and a brand new life transformed by You.

Holy Spirit, open new doors for me. Bring new relationships to me and place me within a loving and godly community for my continual healing. As Your son/daughter, I have been made worthy of Your time, attention, sacrifice and personal destiny. I am Yours.

Discussion on how the church can respond to matters of sexual identity is provided in Appendix 3.

REFLECT AND DISCUSS

1. How might it be dangerous to self-approve of every feeling we experience?

2. When we hold a truth that goes against culture, how do we maintain the courage to not compromise?

3. How are you more than your sexual desires, dreams and feelings?

4. What does it mean to you to deny yourself, pick up your cross and to follow Jesus?

5. Of the seven closing reflections toward healing, which one speaks to you the most and why?

Other helpful resources

www.help4families.org – Help, resources and groups for transgenderism and homosexuality.

www.sexchangeregret.com – Help for those persons who regret sex changes.

www.firststone.org – Discipleship and restoration for the sexually broken.

www.celebraterecovery.com – A Christian 12-step program for recovery from multiple addictions.

www.faithfulandtrue.com – Excellent site and podcast available from the late Dr. Mark Laaser.

ENDNOTES

1. "Answers to Your Questions for a Better Understanding of Sexual Orientation and Homosexuality," American Psychological Association (Washington, DC: APA, 2008).

2–3. Samuel Smith, "Gender-Confused Kids Are Being Experimented on With Hormone Therapy: Experts," *The Christian Post*, June 21, 2017, https://www.christianpost.com/news/gender-confused-kids-are-being-experimented-on-with-hormone-therapy-experts.html.

4. "The National Longitudinal Study of Adolescent to Adult Health (Add Health)," RTI International, https://www.rti.org/impact/national-longitudinal-study-adolescent-adult-health-add-health.

5. Samuel Smith, "No Scientific Evidence that People Are Born Gay or Transgender Johns Hopkins Researchers Say," *The Christian Post*, August 22, 2016, https://www.christianpost.com/news/no-scientific-evidence-that-people-are-born-gay-or-transgender-johns-hopkins-researchers-say.html.

6. Samuel Smith, "Gender-Confused Kids Are Being Experimented on With Hormone Therapy: Experts," *The Christian Post*, June 21, 2017, https://www.christianpost.com/news/gender-confused-kids-are-being-experimented-on-with-hormone-therapy-experts.html.

7. Andrew T. Walker, *God and the Transgender Debate: What Does the Bible Actually Say about Gender Identity?* (Surrey, England: The Good Book Company, 2017).

8–10. "Transformed: A Brief Biblical and Pastoral Introduction to Understanding Transgender in a Changing Culture (London: Evangelical Alliance, 2018), https://www.eauk.org/assets/files/downloads/Transformed.pdf.

11. Stephanie Roy, "Christian Bioethical Approaches to Gender Reassignment Surgery: Understanding Opposition and Retrieving the Body-Soul Complex," *The Student Journal of LMU Theological Studies* 2, no. 2 (May 2020).

12. Glenn Stanton, *Loving My (LGBT) Neighbor: Being Friends in Grace and Truth* (Chicago: Moody Publishers, 2014).

13. Jim Anderson, *Unmasked: Exposing the Cultural Sexual Assault* (Franklin, TN: Carpenter's Son Publishing, 2012).

14. Henri J. M. Nouwen, *You Are the Beloved: Daily Meditations for Spiritual Living* (New York: Convergent Books, 2017).

15–17. Scott Newgent, "We Need Balance When It Comes to Gender Dysphoric Kids. I Would Know," *Newsweek*, February 19, 2021.

I am reconciled to God through Christ who also gave me the ministry of reconciliation.

II Corinthians 5:18

I am chosen, a royal priest, God's special possession, out of darkness and into his wonderful light.

I Peter 2:9

Christ bore my sins on the cross and by his wounds I have been healed.

I Peter 2:24

He has considered me faithful and appointed me to his service.

I Timothy 1:12

PART 4: PERSONALIZING IDENTITY
CHAPTER TWELVE

My Story

Identity is a prison you can never escape, but the way to redeem your past is not to run from it, but to try to understand it, and use it as a foundation to grow. — Jay Z

When faced with a challenge, happy families, like happy people, just add a new chapter to their life story that show them overcoming the hardship. This skill is particularly important for children, whose identity tends to get locked in during adolescence. — Bruce Feller

I grew up in a home of domestic violence. Clearly, homes such as these are chaotic, unpredictable; they lack security and the ability to build healthy identity. They easily become homes in which people are just trying to survive. You never really know what might come next.

I became more and more of a loner while growing up. I lived in the country, three miles outside our small town. I loved that setting. That locale afforded me the opportunity to ride my bike for miles and miles along country roads with little to no traffic. It allowed me to be at "the creek" for hours on end fishing, camping, constructing rafts or ice skating in the winter months. The acres of woods behind our home gave me endless opportunity to explore, hike and camp. In fact, for a number of years, I had a permanent tent set up in order to spend weekends in the woods rather than in my home.

All these pleasing places were escapes from the fighting, yelling, swearing and violence of my home. How does a young child adapt to such a family life, only to think that it is normal? Because it was the late 1950s and 60s, we did not share anything about our home life to our teachers or even extended family members. Who would believe us? We were just kids. There was no domestic violence hotline in those days and, even if there was, who would call it for fear of even more retribution and rage to follow?

So, I ran. I ran away on my bike, to the creek, into the woods or to a neighboring farm helping them to bale hay, feed the animals or do any chore they would allow me to participate in. But on the weeknights or weekends I was unable to escape? These times were especially terrifying. Laying in my bed awake for hours on end with the covers drawn up tightly around my neck—even in the heat of summer with an unairconditioned room—was the only protection I knew from what was going on outside my bedroom.

When I turned fifteen, I lied about my age on a work application and acquired a job as a dishwasher at a local, small, private hospital. I illegally rode my motorcycle without a driver's license or license plate to work or caught a ride with my sister. I loved my job and loved the hours I was away from my home. Because work was one of my escapes, I developed a strong work ethic that has carried me throughout life.

Insecurity and the lack of any identity plagued me. I never knew who I was, how I fit in, why I existed or if I even wanted to or should exist. Many times, I contemplated the thought of running away on the train that meandered through the field below my home near the creek. Where would I go? Where would I end up? How would I support myself? I really didn't care as long as I was not at home.

In the home of an insecure, angry abuser, name calling is a form of communication. That communication is full of negative messages like, "You, you'll never amount to anything," or "Why can't you be like so-and-so" or "Could you be anymore stupid...dumb...worthless?" When a parent is struggling with their own lost sense of security and identity, they certainly cannot build it within their child. A child is not able to correctly interpret whose esteem and identity—whether his own or that of the adult—is the issue. Children will interpret all those negative projections onto themselves over and over until they become beliefs, sometimes lifelong beliefs.

In Michelle Obama's book *Becoming*, she is quoted as saying, "If you don't get out there and define yourself, you'll be quickly and inaccurately defined by others."[1] While the part about being defined by others seems to ring true enough, if left solely to ourselves to define ourselves by ourselves, based only on feelings from historical lies or wrong foundations, then defining one's self may be a greater disaster or detriment than having another defining us. That is, another person might actually think of us more highly than we think of ourselves.

Henri Nouwen wrote in stark contrast in a devotional titled "The 'Ifs' that Enslave Me," "As long as I keep running about asking 'Do you love me? Do you really love me?' I give all power to the voices of the world and put myself in bondage because the world is filled with 'ifs.' The world says: 'Yes, I love you if you have a good education, ... sell much and buy much.' There are endless 'ifs' hidden in the world's love. These 'ifs' enslave me, since it is impossible to respond adequately to all of them. The world's love is and always will be conditional. As long as I keep looking for my true self in the world of conditional love, I will remain 'hooked' to the world—trying, failing, and trying again. It is a world that fosters addictions because what it offers cannot satisfy the deepest craving of my heart."[2]

My Mimi

The opportunity to stay with my grandmother was always a welcome solace. My grandmother, Mimi, loved God. She would pray with me and sing to me. She always accepted me, my questions and my insecurities. She always validated my existence. I remember one time she told me, "I know life is not normal at your home, but you always have me and my home. I love you."

My grandfather, Mimi's husband, died at a young age of a heart attack. She, a long-time widow, was the most kind, generous, loving, godly woman I knew. I loved her home and everything about it. It represented peace to me. It was love and acceptance to me and it was life to me. It was her love and my mother's love that gave me every ounce of security that could be drawn upon.

But Mimi contracted cancer and died way too early in life. I was only a teenager at the time. I missed her horribly and blamed God for her departure from this earth prematurely. The one person outside the walls of my home who knew my life and who provided safety for me was now permanently gone from my life.

The Vietnam War was on, and I entered the Air Force in the early 1970s to once again run from my home. I loved the education, my new friends, the work and the responsibility. I loved my permanent duty station, states away from my home.

A life-changing event

Before I get too far ahead of myself, the year before leaving to go into the military, I was partying regularly on weekends. I was self-destructing with an "I don't really care" attitude. My friends were helping me escape my home by providing weekend places to stay and lots of alcohol to drink. I'll spare you all the gory details, but suffice it to say, none of this was helping my identity in a positive way.

When we're struggling to know who we are and why we exist, a sin-filled lifestyle will not take us in the right direction. Yet, self-destructive ways seem to come to us so easily, so naturally. How do we ever think that partying, stunting our personal emotional growth through alcohol or drug use, and hurting loving relationships help in any form or fashion? What makes us think there is anything "normal" about this style of living? Instead, what it does is reinforce how worthless we are, how valueless we are and how unhealthy we are. It accentuates the negative self-hatred that we're continually dealing with and it can become permanently destructive.

I had a friend tell me one time that every single person he had hung out with as a teen or a twenty-something was dead from a drug overdose. Our dysfunctional families, our negative esteem, our lack of identity draw us into this personal nightmare. But, there is a permanent, life-changing way out. Finding this way for myself was literally life-saving.

My senior year

For the two summers before graduation from high school, I was hanging out at the beach. It was there that I heard the gospel for the very first time. A young, blonde-haired girl that I was particularly attracted to went on a date with me and began to talk to me about Jesus. Granted, I attended my local Lutheran church in my home community once in a while, but I never heard the things that this young girl was about to tell me.

She told me I needed a personal relationship with Jesus. She told me He was coming back again. She told me He died on a cross for my salvation. She told me He would change my life if I accepted Him. I did not argue against any of this—because I wanted her. I would tell her, rather manipulatively, that I agreed on all points and that I was cool with God, honestly hoping, all the while, that He was cool with me.

But it was the words of this girl, her passion, her excitement about a living relationship that attracted me to Him within her. I don't really know why, but from somewhere deep in my soul or my spirit, I was hungry for this truth. I was hungry for what was real and I desperately wanted God to be real.

Angry at God

While I was angry at God for my family upbringing, for the death of my grandmother and for just being "missing in action" as a Father, I also had this sense of the reality of Him and His love through Jesus. I guess He was already speaking to my heart and those words from this girlfriend, hours away from my home at the shore, were confirming truth to me.

In time, she sent me a "Dear John" letter. That letter included a gospel tract about "being saved." Oh, how I wanted to be saved, whatever that really meant. How I wanted to escape the reality of my home and family. How I longed to fill the huge void in my life. I didn't know how it would be possible. I simply was not raised with faith outside of my grandmother's words and prayers.

I would read the tract, then throw it down and say to myself, "Oh, I wish" or "Yeah, right...too good to be true." Nights later I would pick it up and read it again. Finally, one night, around midnight, I, with little to no faith, but with huge desire, got down on my knees beside my bed and I prayed, *Jesus, I am not sure if any of this is true. I am not* sure of Your love, but please forgive me of my sin, my hatred for my father, my bitterness, my anger at You and whatever else I need to let go of to receive You into my heart. Please change me!

That night and only that night, for what seemed like a long period of time, there was a very bright light in my room. It was so bright that I had to keep my eyes closed. Even with eyes tightly closed, it seemed to burn throughout my room and quite literally into me. I can't explain it to this day, but I know it was there and it was real. The Bible says that Jesus is the Light of the world and I personally know Him to be that. His light of approval, acceptance, security and love literally and translucently shone in my bedroom that December night. I have never seen it since, but I can testify to you how real and how deeply cleansing it was to me.

A brand-new life

My senior year in high school was not an easy time to become a Christian. But I did everything I could to tell everyone what had happened to me. I was changed and I had an inordinate desire and hunger to read the Bible, to pray, to know Christ, to meet other Christians and to become who I was to become in Him. With whole-hearted zeal, I shared with anyone who would listen to me.

The more I read the Bible, the more I realized what a heavenly Father I actually had. His love, His truth and His Spirit began to penetrate my spirit, soul and body. I truly was a "new creature," with all things new in my life.

And then there was my father

My father hated my new direction. Late one evening he barged into my bedroom and screamed, "I'd rather have you on drugs than believing this Jesus stuff!" He said this at about the same time I was reading in the book of Luke how Jesus prayed from the cross, "Father, forgive them, for they know not what they are doing." I spoke the same prayer for my earthly father: *Father, forgive him, for he knows not what he is saying. He has no frame of reference for what has happened to me. He doesn't understand; the only response he knows is anger. This choice I have made is out of his control.* It would be Jesus in me that would enable me to love my father again with an honest and sincere love. To love when we are not loved or do not feel loved is truly inspired by God.

The depth of Christ's forgiveness to me presses me to forgive my father. It forces the question of what evil occurred in his life through his father and others. What abuses did he suffer and what deep secrets has he suppressed? Out of his wounds he wounds others, even those he loves.

To hate is easy. To disregard and abandon is natural. But to love, to forgive, to have hope for a lost soul is supernatural. As a youth, tormented by his out-of-control rage, I wanted him to die or leave our family, never to be seen again. Now, having known the love of God my Father, I would only long for his redemption. My heart was being healed and that healing resulted in an in-depth healing of who I was and who I was to become. For if I chose to hate, be angry and pursue retribution of my father the remainder of my life, I would be the one suffering, not him. Unforgiveness is certainly a road we can take, but it comes with a heavy emotional, physical and spiritual price. (We will discuss more about parent wounds in chapter 16.)

In Peter Scazzero's book *Emotionally Healthy Spirituality*, he shares valid information from Murray Bowen who is the originator of the term *differentiation*. He discusses differentiation this way: "In families there is a powerful opposition when one member of that system matures and increases his or her level of differentiation. I have seen repeatedly that when anyone makes a change in themselves (becoming their true self in Christ), a few people around them often get upset."

Murray Bowen lists this opposition in three stages:

"Stage one: You are wrong for changing and here are the reasons why.

Stage two: Change back and we will accept you again.

Stage three: If you don't change back, these are the consequences _____."[3]

These words describe amazingly well the differentiation I was feeling, and there were even more changes ahead for me.

The price of love on the cross was too great. I cannot transgress that sacrifice which was made for every person on the earth, including my father. Perhaps I will never forget the pain, the sleepless nights, the many tears, the sadness and the aloneness while growing up, but those things will never dictate or define who I am, how I walk out my life today and who I am becoming. Those experiences will make me a better person, a healthier person and a more determined person who will run to my heavenly Father's arms.

More change

God gave me new friends while I did my best to keep my old ones whom I truly loved and cared about. These new friends began to disciple me in the faith and help me to discover who I really was, why I existed and what the true purpose of my life was. This new creation was being rebuilt from the inside out. My mind was being washed and my spirit cleansed from so many misbeliefs about life and about myself every single day.

It was as if God was saying to me personally, as He did to that 15-year-old counselee, "Regardless of the family you were born into, I so much desired you; therefore, you exist." And, "You are not born again for yourself, but for Me, for My purposes and My new direction for your life." To this day, my wife tells me that she married a "military airplane mechanic," but wow, where we have come in forty-five years by following this Voice in my life is undeniably incredible!

My esteem was rooted in rejection, disappointment, abuse, loneliness and self-hate. To receive the love of God, the redemption of God, the acceptance of God, the approval of God was like receiving a new life narrative with a new mind and a new spirit.

In the book *Alter Ego*, Craig Groeschel writes, "If you're in Christ, it doesn't matter how you feel about yourself. Even if you think, 'I'm not that good,' or 'I'm not that talented,' you need to understand this: You've been made new. You've been remade. You are God's masterpiece, but you're not just some painting that gets hung up on a wall where people can walk by and say 'Oh, that's a beautiful painting.' No, you are God's masterpiece created to grow, serve, and glorify the Artist, who gives you life."[4]

I love how Craig informs us that we are—I am—God's masterpiece. Truths like this will rebuild the wounded, rejected soul. The truth of the Scripture was coming alive to me at this time in my life and was beginning to penetrate with new life and new beliefs.

Scriptures like these helped to rebuild who I was and who I was becoming:

I am now God's child – I John 3:2
I am loved by Christ and freed from my sins – Revelation 1:5
I am the righteousness of God – II Corinthians 5:21

I am free from all condemnation – Romans 8:1
I am free from my past – Philippians 3:13
I am a new creature – II Corinthians 5:17
I am the temple of the Holy Spirit – I Corinthians 6:19
I am reconciled to God – II Corinthians 5:18
I am rescued from the power of darkness – Colossians 1:13
I am accepted by Christ – Romans 15:7
I am healed by the wounds of Jesus – I Peter 2:24
I am not condemned – John 5:24
I have peace with God – Romans 5:1
I am chosen by Him – I Thessalonians 1:4
Christ's truth has set me free – John 8:32
Christ is being formed in me – Galatians 4:19
For freedom Christ has set me free – Galatians 5:1
I have the mind of Christ – I Corinthians 2:16

More biblical truths like these are provided in Appendix 2, *Who I Am in Christ*.

These verses began the work of removing darkness from my soul through His marvelous light found within His Word.

Just like me, you are God's love and passion. He knows what the lies of this world have done to your identity. We were all sinful when our mothers gave birth to us (Psalm 51:5), but we inherited this sin; it was never God's plan for us. You are God's design as Psalm 139 states:

"You know when I sit and when I rise; you perceive my thoughts from afar. You discern my going out and my lying down; you are familiar with all my ways. Before a word is on my tongue you, Lord, know it completely.... Such knowledge is too wonderful for me, too lofty for me to attain. Where can I go from your Spirit? Where can I flee from your presence? ... If I say, 'Surely the darkness will hide me and the light become night around me,' even the darkness will not be dark to you; the night will shine like the day, for darkness is as light to you. For you created my inmost being; you knit me together in my mother's womb. I praise you because I am fearfully and wonderfully made; your eyes saw my unformed body; all the days ordained for me were written in your book before one of them came to be. How precious to me are your thoughts, God! How vast is the sum of them! Were I to count them, they would outnumber the grains of sand" (Psalm 139:2-18).

Have you ever known such affirmation as that psalm pronounces? What powerful, security-filled, identity-producing words the Father has spoken over you. He knows you, so He knows exactly how to rebuild you. He knows how to do "frame off" reconstruction in your life. Before you ever uttered a word in this life, He knew you completely. There is no dark season of life in which He is not with you, loving you and giving you light. Light draws our attention. It is attractive, while darkness is a search for covering up our sin. Come to this Light, the Light I saw in my bedroom the night I asked Jesus into my life. That Light will not disappoint.

More stories of real-life transformation are ahead in the next chapter. I hope you will identify with them in some way and receive further encouragement for your own personal story of change and growth.

REFLECT AND DISCUSS

1. Can you identify any points in which you know God was showing Himself to you in your childhood, even when you were not looking for Him?

2. Was there a person in your life that was a solace to you? Have you been able to thank him or her for their love?

3. Have you been able to identify things that were destructive to your identity and then things that were positive in rebuilding your identity?

ENDNOTES

1. Michelle Obama, *Becoming* (New York: Viking, an Imprint of Penguin Books, 2018).

2. Henri J. M. Nouwen, "The 'Ifs' That Enslave Me," *You Are the Beloved: Daily Meditations for Spiritual Living* (New York: Convergent Books, 2017).

3. Peter Scazzero, *Emotionally Healthy Spirituality* (Grand Rapids, MI: Zondervan, 2014), 67–68.

4. Craig Groeschel, *Alter Ego: Becoming Who God Says You Are* (Grand Rapids, MI: Zondervan, 2013), 36.

I am the temple of the Holy Spirit.

I Corinthians 6:19

I am crucified with Christ
nevertheless I live.

Galatians 2:20

I have been given all things
that pertain to life.

II Peter 1:3

I have been blessed with
every spiritual blessing.

Ephesians 1:3

CHAPTER THIRTEEN

You Are Uniquely You

Stop letting others decide who you are. — Dan Mohler

Be who you are and say what you feel because those who mind don't matter and those who matter don't mind.
— Dr. Seuss

Her little body laid in the middle of the road with what looked like her mother's dark gray coat over it. Her mother knelt alongside crying and stroking her bloody hair. My wife and I were on our way home from my office and we came across this horrific accident. Apparently, the little girl's snow sled had strayed directly into oncoming traffic on a busy road.

The next day as I drove by that same farm, I began to wonder something. What would the mother take in the place of her daughter? I mean, she owned a beautiful Lancaster County, Pennsylvania farm. Would she agree to the farm being paid off in exchange for letting her daughter die? Would they agree to brand new tractors and equipment in a switch for letting their daughter go?

I am certain that the answer from those parents, the mother in particular, would be, "Take the farm; give me back my daughter!" At that moment it would be a quick and easy decision: life over stuff. Life over farms. Life over security and life over any sense of identity in any earthly thing. Anything one might be looking to for identity would fade in light of such a loss.

Fortunately, we do not experience such loss on a daily basis, but we do make daily decisions based on our history, our present life experiences and what we see as our future.

Decisions we make

God has created us with the capacity to think within three realms: past, present and future. The memory capacity of our brains is simply amazing; it provides the knowledge we need from past experiences that enables us to make decisions today.

Just imagine what life would be like if we lacked memory. We would not know how to drive home from work. We would not know or be able to identify our spouse in the morning when we wake up. We would have to start each new day reading a memory log from the day before: who we are, where we live, where we work or go to school. Life would function so differently. We can conclude memory is not only necessary for life, it provides so much wonderful meaning to life.

If someone asks you where you would like to go to dinner, you can look back into history and reply, "I don't know, but we're never going to the diner again. They tried to poison us with the last meal we ate there." Or, you can stop and ask yourself what you're presently hungry for, making your decision based on the present. Lastly, you can make a decision that connects to the future, which might go something like this: "Let's try the new Italian restaurant because I'm looking for a place to celebrate our anniversary next month." This is an example of a present decision based upon a future desire.

Influence from our future, present and past

Financial decisions are made this way, too. Making a financial decision based on the future means you can see your present income being set aside for an investment that will provide a return when you retire. As well, you can place extra cash on your present mortgage, because your goal for the future is to pay your thirty-year mortgage off in twenty years. It takes a present-realm action to realize a completed goal in the future. Regardless, you must be thinking of the future in order to reach your goal.

Having a financial mindset for the present only is short-sighted. It conveys that if I have enough food and shelter for today alone, life is satisfactory. There is no concern for tomorrow. I regularly visit a foreign nation whose culture primarily works for today's provision and takes no thought for tomorrow. This mentality engages a specific mindset that can bring harm to any positive change for the future.

Living only for today also makes you susceptible to marketing strategies that are designed to create dissatisfaction within you. If they are successful, you will be coaxed to purchase the new and improved version of whatever is being sold, without thought of how the decision will affect you in the future. Many cars today will run well for 150,000-plus miles so they do not need to be quickly replaced. Yet, when the newest model and latest gadgets are showcased, that car becomes so enticing. It makes your old model look and feel antiquated, thus promoting feelings of dissatisfaction.

Most persons who make financial decisions solely for the present have no savings account and nothing to fall back on in difficult times. This person lives paycheck to paycheck without a thought of loss of a job or any unexpected catastrophe.

Making financial decisions with only the past in mind is like driving your car backwards. Eventually, you will run into something or someone. If our standard of decision-making is constantly filtered through our histories, we will rarely take risks.

For example, if you choose to never invest in stocks again because a past investment lost you money, then you will certainly never make money in the stock market in the future, even though many do. You are allowing your financial past to dictate your present and your future decisions.

Every day, you are making decisions affecting your future and how you will live your life. You are also making decisions impacting your long-term security and identity.

Consequences of poor decision-making

When a young person starts experimenting with drugs to numb the pain of a past or present hurt, they are risking the possibility of destroying their future. The decisions they make about drug use today, usually without a second thought, can permanently change their future.

Depression is most often connected to our histories. We allow our past to determine our present state of mind, which has a bearing on how we see our future. Anxiety, or the fear of something in our future, is frequently determined by our self-imposed fear or dread of something that has not even occurred. Obviously depression and anxiety can be very complicated, so I am not attempting to make them seem simplistic. What I am alluding to is that present feeling or thought is often based upon past experience and how we interpret that past. Or, it can be based upon a future fear when thinking of the possibility of a yet-to-occur event.

Sowing and reaping

The Bible says what we sow, we reap. (See Galatians 6:7, 8.) Think about this concept. The type of seed that I plant today determines the return I will have on it tomorrow. If I desire a certain crop in the future, then I need to sow that specific seed today. No single farmer expects to reap where they have not sown, but every farmer fully expects to reap where they have sown. You may expect to be a millionaire one day in the future, but if you do nothing and place no effort toward that goal today, you will never see it. It is easy to then become deceived into thinking you will win the lottery or inherit that million, but without earning it. The Scriptures describe this type of gain as ill-gotten treasure. (See Proverbs 10:2.)

Do you want to live in health in your latter years? Take measures today to exercise and eat healthy because when reaching tomorrow, today will be the past. Do you desire to be free of pain from your past? Then do something about it today and forgive those who have hurt you and bless those who have cursed you.

Unfortunately, I experienced a lot of cavities in my teeth as a child. My family did not use toothpaste with fluoride in it. Fluoride wasn't even marketed in those days. My trips to the dentist were fear-filled and excruciating. Today, I pay the price of dealing with crowns to save my teeth. My past dental care affects my present oral condition and will continue to affect my future.

You just cannot separate these three: the past, the present and the future. But you can start making decisions in alignment with God's Word and His direction for your life. A better decision today means a better outcome tomorrow. A destructive decision today brings pain in our future.

Take the decision of divorce. When we choose to end our marriage, we can be deceived into thinking our pain will be over when the marriage is over. More than likely, it will not be. We will continue to face and possibly interact with our ex-spouse for many years to come. We might be dealing with children who go back and forth between parents. We might struggle financially. It could take us years to recover from the pain of a divorce when a marriage of oneness has been ripped apart.

We may desire immediate pain-free solutions, but they do not exist in the real world. Our decisions not only have a lasting effect on us but also on important people in our life.

Stress and worry

Are you a worrier? I mean, does your mind immediately go to the exercise of worry when you are faced with an unknown? Or, do you respond to a worrisome issue by going to your heavenly Father in prayer and trust? One response is trusting and relying upon yourself and your capacity to worry (needing to solve the issue yourself) and the other is trusting God and His capacity to intervene, both in the here-and-now and the future. Philippians 4:6, 7 reminds us to not be anxious, and if we'll petition God along with giving thanks, the peace of God will guard our hearts and minds. Peace does not follow worry; it follows prayer and trusting God, literally giving our worry to God. (See also Psalm 37:1-8.)

Self-spoken vows

Have you ever experienced something in your past and then either externally or internally responded with the expression, *I'll never let that happen again*? Or perhaps your response was, *No one will ever get close enough to hurt me that deeply in the future.* By doing so, you are literally speaking words over yourself that inhibit your present and your future. These words can become spoken vows, bringing destruction to future relationships and yourself.

When you repeat the words, "I will never… again," you are attempting to shield yourself from future hurt, but what you are actually doing is speaking curse-filled words over your present and your future. In other words, those present-day words spoken from broken, hurtful relationships in your past have a profound effect upon your future connections.

From victim to victor

Victims remain victims because they harbor unforgiveness that has turned into bitterness. Victims live out this bitterness on an ongoing basis by reliving the hurt and the pain and then telling themselves the person or persons who hurt them, who abused them or who took advantage of them deserve justice and do not deserve their forgiveness.

It may sound harsh, but victims remain victims by living in their victimization—it keeps them in the past. Victims do not need to change to create a better future, because we enable victims today to stay victims. Too often, victims view themselves as powerless people, powerless to change and create a better future. Nothing could be further from the truth.

I have a close friend; we'll call her Mia (not her real name). Mia had a highly chaotic childhood. She described her family as "separated," with her parents living together separately. Her brother was in and out of foster care. Her older sister left home early to escape the abuse and later to live a "hippie" lifestyle. Meanwhile, Mia lived on the streets, in and out of friends' houses, with her sister, or family from age thirteen on.

Her father would come home every night from his business and drink a fifth of whiskey. Her mother would drink alcohol in her bedroom and take prescription drugs all day long. Eventually, every night would escalate into a brawl between her father and mother. It became physical and scary to Mia.

"One night after midnight, when I was around age seven or eight," Mia told me, "I woke up and followed my mother into our kitchen. I watched her grab a large butcher knife then I followed her to the bedroom where my father slept. I saw her raise her arm in the air with the knife in hand. I was terrified; I began to tug on her nightgown as hard as I could, and scream. My father abruptly woke up and ran from the bedroom as she moved to stab him. She missed and instead sunk the knife into the wooden bedroom door while her hand slid down the knife blade from the impact and cut her deeply. There was blood everywhere. The police or the fire department would show up night after night to our home."

Mia said, "I felt so much shame within my neighborhood; everyone knew who we were and what we were." She told me, "I had to take control and I used my anger to do so. I decided that I had to be the one that everyone followed because I longed for the attention. My identity was lost in this dysfunctional family and I was desperately trying to survive. At age twelve I started the life of drinking and drugs, experimenting with marijuana, to the dabbling of LSD and cocaine, which eventually became my drug of choice. Unfortunately, I also lost my virginity at that age."

Mia began to realize the attention she received from boys, many boys, brought on and reinforced some mutually consensual sexual encounters. But it also brought on many who took advantage of her, especially when she was high or drinking heavily. Mia shared, "I wrongly equated male attention through sex with acceptance and love."

"But some of the most traumatic moments for me," Mia described, "were sleeping in my mother's bed night after night. She used me as a buffer to keep my father from sexually assaulting her. She kept me close to her through the night which felt creepy and yucky, feelings so undesired. My home and my family were a place of defilement for me. There was no nurturing touch, no safety, no comfort and no faith."

There was one highlight in Mia's upbringing: the godly neighbor lady who lived in the home behind her home. There Mia heard the gospel for the first time as the woman shared Bible stories on her flannelgraph board and then shared cookies with Mia and her friends. Mia relayed, "One day I decided to ask Jesus into my life. I would go home that day and many days thereafter asking God, begging God to change my family. I realize since that time, my life was spared so many more times by the hand of God."

By age sixteen Mia was a cocaine addict, missed a lot of school and was attending parties with rock-n-roll stars in southern California, using heroin. She said, "I would wake up in the morning after a party somewhere, not knowing whose house I was in, how I got there or how I would get home." From this activity, she contracted hepatitis B and almost died in the hospital. Once again, she knew God's hand was on her and giving her life. "I did not want to be a drug addict. I tried to become healthy and only party on weekends."

Eventually Mia discovered a place of prayer in her life and began asking God to help her. She started to see glimpses of God's love for her. Her story continues, "At age twenty-two, I met my husband to be and we partied our way into marriage. Someone told me around this time that I was becoming just like my mother, and that scared me, because I was determined not to become my mother."

"I began Alcoholics Anonymous (AA) meetings and then Al-Anon meetings in an attempt to become sober and deal with my family issues, but after several years found myself wondering if this is all there is."

Mia finds a new identity

"One day I turned on the TV and began to listen to a Christian talk show," Mia recalled. "They were speaking about angels and the supernatural. I was so drawn to the conversation. I couldn't stop watching. I watched day after day and then got my husband to watch with me. One day we called in to the phone counselors and they recommended a local church that also had counseling. In counseling I began to confront the many lies I believed or was led to believe as a child growing up. What really began to change was my perception of God and what He desired for me versus what I desired for myself."

Mia described herself as stained, with her identity, her soul and her spirit so imprinted upon by all the abuse from her past. "I believed that I was bad. All the lies reinforced the false identity I lived with. Growing up in an alcoholic, abusive home left me with a deeply flawed and distorted sense of identity. I had no understanding of what a healthy foundation for life was. My needs simply became the extension of what others needed from me or wanted me to be. This set me up to look for love and validation in all the wrong places and just perpetuated my distorted identity."

She went on, "God unraveled lie after lie and the deep mistrust that came from continual sexual abuse. I discovered that I trusted no one but myself." As each lie was confronted, God was also revealing to Mia truth from His Word. She said that a major factor in her healing was being led by the Holy Spirit into truth so that she could hear her heavenly Father's heart toward her.

"I began to believe what God was saying to me about me," Mia explained. "I felt His presence, but mostly I felt His love—His unconditional love—for me." She described herself as "frozen" and that her heavenly Father was melting away the emotionally dead parts of herself. Particularly powerful was when Mia heard God say to her, "Will you let Me love your heart? I will never abuse you or your heart. I will not force your will and I will not trespass. Will you let Me go to the deeper places of your heart?"

"I am no longer a victim. The more I let God love me, the more I comprehend that," Mia said. "There is an 'old Mia,' but Jesus took those old hurts, abuses and victimizations to the cross for me. The healing process from being a victim to a victor has been a journey of finding truth. The journey to finding my true identity has come as a result of pursuing my relationship with Christ, growing in my understanding and relationship with the Holy Spirit, forgiving those who hurt me and allowing His truth to reveal to me who I truly am."

One of the most profound things Mia said to me in our interview was, "My failures no longer define me; Christ's redemption now defines me."

Revisiting forgiveness—past, present, and future

One of the most significant ways to be a victor is through forgiveness. To forget your past is not humanly possible. The more traumatic an event was, the less chance of forgetting. But forgiving is a choice you can make that releases you and the one who hurt you so that you can live victoriously in the present and the future. Isaiah reminds us to forget the past, to not dwell on the former things (Isaiah 43:18, 19). It is not possible to clearly see tomorrow through the cloudy lens of the past.

"But one thing I do (present): Forgetting what is behind (past) and straining toward what is ahead (future), I press on toward the goal to win the prize for which God has called me heavenward in Christ Jesus (present/future)" (Philippians 3:13, 14, additions mine).

Jesus told us, "For if you forgive men when they sin against you (past/present), your heavenly Father will also forgive you (present/future). But if you do not forgive men their sins (past/present), your Father will not forgive your sins (present/future)" (Matthew 6:14, 15, additions mine).

We cannot just forget our past or pretend that it did not happen. Yet, we dare not walk in bitterness and unforgiveness. Forgiveness has medicinal benefits; it is a prescription directly from heaven for our freedom. But lest we get it wrong, forgiveness is not totally based on our decision; it is based on what Christ has already accomplished on the cross. He bore our sins as we crucified Him. Forgiveness is what He did for us: past, present and future.

You have been forgiven even though you deserved to die for your sin. Not one of us would escape judgment. We have all done enough wrong to spend eternity without Him. But forgiveness reflects who God is. Jesus was God's example in the flesh of forgiveness even as He hung on the cross.

When we withhold forgiveness from another, we actually withhold forgiveness from ourselves; we are the ones who suffer. Unforgiveness can cause stress, sleeplessness, anxiety, depression, high blood pressure, stomach issues, rapid heartbeat, and much more. So many trips to the doctor today are a result of emotional breakdown. If left uncared for, these can eventually lead to physical breakdowns as the physical body attempts to absorb the negative emotions generated by unforgiveness. Past hurts will eventually affect present mind, will and emotions, leaving us with an unsure future.

True forgiveness brings freedom

True forgiveness allows us to live in freedom today because we no longer hold onto anything from our past. Forgiveness is not a natural act; it is an act of God in our lives. It is letting go of revenge or the thought of getting even. Forgiveness is both immediate and long term. Even when we forgive, getting free from the feelings of pain, loss, anger or desire for retribution can take some time.

Henri Nouwen said, "[Forgiveness] demands of me that I step over that wounded part of my heart that feels hurt and wronged and that wants to stay in control and put a few conditions between me and the one whom I am asked to forgive."[1]

Emotional wounds

Lastly, true forgiveness will eventually allow me to forget the wrong. Deep wounds can lose their sting long before the mind forgets. When we suffer a deep cut, we tend to it immediately. We might require an X-ray, get shots to numb the pain, and then it is sewn up. Antibiotics are administered, a tetanus shot is certain, and the wound is watched for weeks to come. When it comes to emotional wounds, however, we often administer a little bit of, "Oh, it's not very deep, it doesn't hurt, and it doesn't need any spiritual attention" and expect things to be fine. We could not be more wrong.

Wounds—any wounds—need attention. Dr. Jesus is the best when it comes to healing deeply because, with His touch, one can eventually forget there ever was a wound. That physical cut soon fades to be merely a scar. In time, even the scar could disappear. The very memory of that emotional wound can disappear through the healing cross of Calvary.

Forgiveness is *presently* acting upon a price that was paid in the *past*, so that we can experience freedom *today* and in our *future*. As Corrie ten Boom faced her tormentor, we too can face a new day today through releasing past torments. We will experience a bright hope-filled *present* and *future*.

This very thing is described and written about from a close friend. Here is her story.

A healing story

"I remember giving my life to God on July 3, 1979 at twelve years of age. Things were difficult at home. All I knew was that I was being told God cared about that, and if I followed Him, He would help me feel better.

"Looking back, I cannot fault a twelve-year-old girl for being so self-centered as to enter a relationship purely for what I could get out of it.

"I am not unfamiliar with the burning questions of identity we all encounter. Perhaps, as a mother of five children who are now adults and as a board-certified health and well-being coach, I have seen this struggle in others more intimately than most. But what consistently confounds people about this concept is they tend to look inward when wanting to answer the question of identity. There is nothing wrong with examining ourselves. In fact, I would suggest that this needs to be done daily to keep us growing. But that is not our identity.

"The only way we can really understand who we are is to completely remove ourselves from our own limited, fickle, fallible filter and instead view ourselves through the 20/20 lenses of who God says we are. Not just who we were created to be (future tense), but who we are (present tense), whether we are walking that out in our lives or not. This view provides a full perspective into who we are as individuals.

"No one has ever been, or ever will be, created like me. That is a powerful, beautiful, joyous fact that we all can claim for ourselves. This gives great meaning to my life and provides satisfaction. But again, it is not my identity. My identity is being God's own child, a joint heir with Jesus, a new creation, forgiven, sanctified, holy, and many more things spoken over me by the Creator. I am not going to question Him, because, well, He's God. His identity is love and more.

Because of Christ's work on the cross, my identity is defined by this wondrous Being.

"This is what I can depend on when in the valleys of despair or the highest mountains of joy. If I were to continue to look inward when trying to negotiate difficult seasons of life, thinking the answer could be found in some yet-undiscovered part of me, I would continue to spiral downward. However, when I instead assume the perspective of God's given identity, I have a structure for hope. Truth overlays the questions that plague me in my misery. I have a scaffold of hopeful, positive, amazing things to help me extricate myself from my situation. Identity is perhaps the greatest challenge each individual faces as they mature."

This story illustrates exactly what we have been talking about. The statement, "The only way we can really understand who we are is to completely remove ourselves from our own limited, fickle, fallible filter and instead view ourselves through the 20/20 lenses of who God says we are" is so true. Yes, as explained, our identity can be found in being God's own child, a joint heir with Jesus, forgiven, sanctified and holy.

This reminds me of words in Ephesians 2 that speak to identity so profoundly. They are the basis for identity. From The Passion Translation of the Bible:

"And his fullness fills you, even though you were once like corpses, dead in your sins and offenses. It wasn't that long ago that you lived in the religion, customs, and value of this world, obeying the dark ruler of the earthly realm who fills the atmosphere with his authority, and works diligently in the hearts of those who are disobedient to the truth of God. The corruption that was in us from birth was expressed through the deeds and desires of our self-life. We lived by whatever natural cravings and thoughts our minds dictated, living as rebellious children subject to God's wrath like everyone else.

"But God still loved us with such great love. He is so rich in compassion and mercy. Even when we were dead and doomed in our many sins, he united us into the very life of Christ and saved us by his wonderful grace! He raised us up with Christ the exalted One, and we ascended with him into the glorious perfection and authority of the heavenly realm, for we are now co-seated as one with Christ!

"Throughout the coming ages we will be the visible display of the infinite riches of his grace and kindness, which was showered upon us in Jesus Christ. For by grace you have been saved by faith. Nothing you did could ever earn this salvation, for it was the love gift from God that brought us to Christ! So no one will ever be able to boast, for salvation is never a reward for good works or human striving.

"We have become his poetry, a re-created people that will fulfill the destiny he has given each of us, for we are joined to Jesus, the Anointed One. Even before we were born, God planned in advance our destiny and the good works we would do to fulfill it!"

These authoritatively eloquent words connect with our past identity, our present identity and our future identity and destiny. There is no authority greater than God's Word when speaking directly to our security and our identity.

Even though we were "dead in our sins," no one was created to be a criminal or a drug addict. No one was created to be a failure. Although we came from a dark place and a place of disobedience, we are no longer defined by those things. While we were "corrupt" from birth, we are no longer seen as corrupt. Even in that state, we were loved by our Creator and His grace was toward us.

These words we just read, "We have become his poetry, a re-created people that will fulfill the destiny he has given each of us" are written to and over each one of us. You are His "poetry." You have been "re-created" to fulfill His destiny through you. Your identity is not earned. It is not mentally assented to. It is not mastered over time. Your identity is given to you by your heavenly Father.

You are uniquely you!

REFLECT AND DISCUSS

1. Can you give examples of decisions made based on the past, the present and imaginations of the future?

2. Can you share an example of sowing something negative and then sowing something positive? Can you relate the differing outcomes of those two?

3. How has forgiving someone brought healing to you?

4. How are emotional wounds different from physical wounds?

5. What specifically speaks to you when reading Ephesians 2:1-10?

ENDNOTE

1. Henri Nouwen, "Divine Forgiveness," Henri Nouwen Society, October 8, https://henrinouwen.org/meditation/divine-forgiveness.

I have been given fullness in Christ.

Colossians 2:10

I am seated with Christ in
heavenly realms.

Ephesians 2:6

I am qualified to share in the
inheritance of the kingdom of light.

Colossians 1:12

I am more than a conqueror.

Romans 8:37

CHAPTER FOURTEEN

Is Your Identity
for Sale?

*Nothing of me is original. I am the combined effort of every-
one I've ever known.* — Chuck Palahniuk, *Invisible Monsters*

*The more isolated and disconnected we are, the more shat-
tered and distorted our self-identity.* — Erwin McManus

*If you don't deal with your demons, your demons
will deal with you.* — Ben Affleck

My wife and I were speaking to a group of more than
thirty senior high youth. They were passionate, hungry,
open, teachable, vulnerable and enthusiastically smiling as
we taught. We spoke about life mission, boundaries, identity,
pornography, priorities and praying for a life mate. We were
straightforward and honest. They listened intently.

As I observed these kids, I thought about the pressure they
are under. I thought of how they have encountered pornography, sex, drugs, broken families, raunchy TV and movies,
and peer pressure—lots of peer pressure. I wondered, "How
do they cope in a world so different from the world I lived in
when I was their age?" And then this frightening question
dawned on me, "Will they sell their identity?"

It was a church youth group. They will soon head to college, technical school or enter the work force. How often
will they be tempted to give up on their faith? What college
professors will tell them Christianity is for the weak and the

brainless? What young lady will attempt to seduce one of these boys or vice versa? Which ones will sell their identity and which ones will hold onto their Christ-centered esteem?

Quickly the answer came to me. It will be you and me who make a difference in their lives. The adults, the parents, the youth leaders, the teachers, their older siblings and grandparents in their lives will touch them, love them, be a godly example to them, pray for and with them and visit them when they are off to college. We will text them, email them and even snail mail them to encourage their faith. We will send them books and articles that will help to protect their identity, and we will speak life to them. We will tell them they are accepted, of value to us and to God. We will challenge them to live righteously and hold them accountable to the truths they have been taught.

And why will we do this? Because they are the next generation to lead, to marry and to have children. If we do not tell them the truth about who and whose they are, we will lose them; their identity will suffer irreparable damage.

The Ben Affleck story

Movie star Ben Affleck grew up in Boston with his brother, Casey. His father was an alcoholic and at age eleven his parents separated and then divorced. His father, Ben states, "was scary to live with." He revealed, "He would get angry at things I didn't understand." From his history, Ben presently feels that "the children pay for the sins of their parents.... We carry a generational burden."

It was a teacher, Ben recalls, who spoke life over him and into him. In the midst of those tumultuous years, that teacher affirmed him, affirmed his talent, spoke encouragement and made him feel secure. During Ben's recovery from his own bout with alcoholism, Ben remembered those words often.[1]

Believing words of affirmation

I was sharing with some high school youth about developing a God-esteem. After the meeting, a young man came to me and opened up about his life struggles. He was trying to follow God, but at the same time was seeing more inadequacies, more stumbling and more loss in his life than anything else. I listened and then offered to pray for him.

Something unexpected happened during that prayer. God told me to tell him that one day he would earn lots and lots of money and that in order to live for Christ, be a good husband and father and earn that kind of money, he would need to clearly know and understand who he was in Christ.

Years later I was attending a wedding of my son's best friend far from our home area. The wife of another friend of the groom approached me and began to share who she was married to. I did not remember or recognize her husband from the story, but then she said, "You met with him in Lancaster, PA, listened to him after a meeting he was attending and took the time to pray with him." She continued, "When you prayed you said something about his need to be secure and find his esteem in God because one day, he would be very wealthy." Now, I vaguely remembered this young man.

She went on to describe so many amazing things about this man she is married to. She then said, "We were on our way here to the wedding when his trip was interrupted by his company sending a limousine to pick him up for an important meeting. This happens a lot. He has a well-paying job in which he makes huge decisions that affect the stock market."

How could we ever know when we just might have the opportunity to speak into the life of another, especially a young person who is struggling? How will we respond in a healthy way if we ourselves do not know health?

Jesus took a group of twelve

In Luke 5:1-11, Jesus is standing by the lake teaching. The crowd is growing. Jesus sees two boats that just happen to be by the water's edge. He climbs into one of them. The owner was washing his nets.

These fishermen most likely had fathers and grandfathers who were fishermen. It was their work and their business. Fishing was not only their livelihood; most times they smelled like fish, cleaned fish, sold fish and ate fish. They could identify species of fish; they were grounded in "fishology." Fishing could easily have been their identity.

Jesus got into the boat owned by Simon. It is understood that He asked Simon if He could borrow him and his boat. Simon must have said, "Yes." Then He asks Simon to push off the shore a bit. There, along with the boat, the nets, and its owner, Jesus teaches people who had gathered.

He finishes his teaching and directs Simon to "put out into the deep water." What He was saying to Simon was this: "You have listened to Me thus far; you had faith to push off shore. Now will you have faith to respond positively and go out to deeper water?"

The request to Simon

What was difficult about this request for Simon? The second request is attached to who Simon was—a fisherman. Jesus told him to lower his nets. Jesus was messing with Simon's profession, Simon's identity, Simon's life career. Fishing was what he knew best. He had been up all night doing it and caught nothing. Can you hear Simon thinking, "Do you, Jesus, know anything about fishing? Why would I even consider lowering my nets when I just fished through midnight shift?" But Simon relents and says, "Because you say so..." Perhaps he was saying, "If there is no catch, it's on

You because You are the one telling me to do this."

Let's look again at what has transpired. A fisherman takes a man on board his boat—a teacher. He says "yes" to pushing off the shore, then says "yes" to going out deeper, then says "yes" to dropping his nets.

This was the point at which Simon Peter's identity transitioned from fishing for fish to fishing for men. Peter just met the One who God planned for him to meet when he was in his mother's womb. Peter met the One who would change his profession, change his identity, change his name, and set a brand-new course for his life. Jesus used the skills Peter had, met him right where he was, and asked only that he obey.

On that day, at that moment, Simon Peter the fisherman became Simon Peter, "the rock," the disciple of Christ. (See Matthew 16:18.) His life and his identity would transition to God's plan and call. Peter would go on to be one of the greatest preachers of the New Testament.

Am I dreaming?

Imagine that you lived two thousand years ago. You just recently heard of this One named Jesus and most of what you have heard was negative. In some strange way, this man and the controversy that surrounds Him intrigues you. You would love to meet Him; you consider making a trip to His town.

The thought leaves you until one day you hear that He is coming. Your town is in an absolute uproar. There are so many questions, so many reports circulating. You wonder why He is coming. Will you see Him? Will He see you? You determine to find your way to the main street in an attempt to catch a closer look. You see the crowds making their way toward you—and here He comes. A strange anxiety and nervousness intensify within you.

Suddenly, He is right there in front of you. He looks your way. You want to look down, but do not know why. In reality, you can't look anywhere but straight at Him. Surprised, He is looking straight at you, eye-to-eye. You don't know how to describe the feeling; His eyes are warm, inviting, questioning. You can't look away. You are lost in His presence and your heart is pounding. He opens His mouth to say something, but it seems to be in slow motion as you hear the words, "Come follow Me." You want to say, "Who, me?" but you can't utter a word. Without thinking, you find one foot going in front of the other and you are, in fact, following Him.

What does He want? Does He need a place to stay, a meal prepared? Along the way, He makes that same statement to others: "Follow Me." It is noticeably not random. His invitations are calculated. No one refuses; they just follow alongside of you. You know something is happening but cannot describe it.

That evening you sit with Him and hear His teaching. You've never heard anything like it. You don't know why you left your family, your home, your profession, but at the same time, you are satisfied and comfortable, knowing this is right. You spend the next three and one-half years with this Man. He knows you like no other. He has taught you by word and by example. He has taught you to pray. He has taught you about His kingdom and demonstrated it time after time, miracle by miracle. You even participated in a few of the miracles yourself.

Recently, He sent you and another disciple out to do what He does. It was exciting. You no longer miss your profession; this is now your life. You have caught something from Him and there is now no other way to live. You want to stay by His side for the rest of your life. There is no other place you desire to be but close to the one you call Master—Jesus.

His latest teaching is strange. It sounds like He is going somewhere that you cannot go. You feel almost rejected, pushed out of the nest. Being thrust into the future without Him is incomprehensible and unimaginable. It's even stranger how He prays these days. His prayer focus has shifted to something about returning to the Father and sending another to be with you and your eleven friends.

You remember that first glance on Main Street and how His eyes met yours. You remember feeling unclean yet accepted, all at the same time. You reflect on so many things now, things that you took for granted over the past three years. "You are going away, Jesus? Where would You be going and why would You be leaving us? We gave everything to follow You. We gave up our businesses and our families. We gave up our homes and our belongings. We gave these things up to follow You and now You leave us and promise another?" You scream inside, "I don't want another; I want You!"

You go off to pray and He goes off to pray. Your friend John records Jesus' prayer and you don't like what you hear. It sounds almost cruel. What will you do now? Where will you go? Will you even like "the other" who He is sending?

Back to reality

Where did Jesus end and His disciples begin? Where did His disciples end and He begin? The relationships were so interwoven. Even though Jesus walked with these men for over three years, there was clarity about who they were and whose they were. Jesus did not request of the Father to let Him bring the disciples with Him or even to stay with them longer. Jesus knew who He was and He knew whose His disciples were. He was not comparing Himself with the Father or competing for the relationships. He was not jealous or possessive of His disciples' relationship with His Father nor did He try to manipulate His Father's plan. Jesus did what He came to do and left earth without His disciples. (See John 17.)

Even though the Father had given these relationships to the Son, the Son respected the boundaries given Him and handed them back to the Father. We see this in John 17:10 where Jesus said, "All I have is yours, and all you have is mine."

We recently experienced our "baby" daughter giving birth to her first child. Today, as parents of two forty-somethings and one thirty-something, we no longer have the influence we once had in their lives. With each milestone our children reach, we give more and more control away. They must accept more and more responsibility and authority. But the framework must be a healthy one: a foundation of security in Jesus. How is that foundation achieved?

A word of knowledge

John chapter four gives an amazing story that gives insight into Jesus' life. It is a story of a woman at a well. She had repeatedly tried to find security and identity in men. After all, she had been married five times. Further, Jesus revealed that the man she was living with was not her husband.

In this conversation, Jesus does not say one condemning word. He said after drinking water, you will be thirsty again, but "whoever drinks the water He gives them will never thirst again…a spring of water welling up to eternal life" (John 4:14).

Jesus tells her He can give her living water, after which she will never thirst again. She yearns for it. When she asked for this water, Jesus told her, "Go, call your husband and come back." Do you notice the dialogue? The woman says, "Give me the water." Jesus answers, "Go get your husband."

Jesus does not answer her request in the typical way. He puts His finger directly on the drawback in her life, the issue, the place where she has missed the mark. This is the one area that is out of control—looking to men for security, identity, and emotional and physical needs. The woman then attempts to redirect Him by talking about a place of worship. Jesus makes it clear that one day all will worship in spirit and in truth. Jesus then reveals Himself to her, not in a parable, but simply by saying, "I am he" (John 4:26). How often was Jesus that straightforward about who He was?

Jesus knew that she had been selling her identity to men, but He also knew an encounter with the One who could give her living water would change her forever. This water would quench her insecurity and her identity thirst. I will never believe this encounter was accidental or random. It was a sovereign confrontation, a meeting that was orchestrated by heaven itself because of the love of God for that one single woman.

To you and to me He says, "I am He." I am your living water. I am your foundation for relationship so that your neediness issues can be resolved. I am your healthy boundary-keeper. I am your esteem. I am your beginning and your end. I am your employer, your real estate agent, your banker and your lawyer. I am your retirement, your health insurance, your accountant. I am your father and your mother. I am your security, and I am your identity. *I am He.*

REFLECT AND DISCUSS

1. Have you considered whose life you are speaking into and the opportunities for ministry that are around you?

2. How is your identity transitioning as it did for Simon Peter?

3. In what ways can you identify with the woman at the well who met Jesus, the true and living water?

ENDNOTE

1. Amy Spencer, "Ben Affleck Talks Raising Kids with His Ex, Facing His Demons and Tackling His Most Personal Movie Role Yet," *Parade*, February 28, 2020, https://parade.com/1001118/amyspencer/ben-affleck-the-way-back.

My righteousness is given to me through faith in Jesus Christ.

Romans 3:22

Once I had no identity, now I am God's.

I Peter 2:10

All who have this hope in Christ purify themselves, just as Christ is pure.

I John 3:3

There is now no condemnation for me in Christ Jesus.

Romans 8:1

CHAPTER FIFTEEN

Your Destiny

My potential is more than can be expressed within the bounds of my race or ethnic identity. — Arthur Ashe

Everyone thinks that a new place or a new identity will jump-start a new life. — Carolyn Leavitt, MD

Eleanor was waiting in line for stamps at her local post office. An acquaintance of hers, who was also standing in line, told her that she could purchase stamps much faster from the stamp machine in the lobby. "I know," said Eleanor, "but the stamp machine won't ask me about my arthritis."

Life is about relationship. Normally, when we experience a conflict, it is not with an object, but rather with a person. When we experience certain joy in our life, that too is connected to a person. Relationship, we might go as far as to say, is the most important thing in life. But as stated throughout this book, all the "earthly" relationships in the world will not provide our identity. Only one relationship can effectively, meaningfully and eternally provide the identity we are all searching for.

I love that Jesus is recorded in John 15 as saying we are His friends (relationship). Then He spoke these amazing words: "You did not choose me, but I chose you and appointed you so that you might go and bear fruit." Jesus chose you!

The psalmist David alluded to this when he wrote, "When I look at the night sky and see the work of your fingers—the moon and the stars you set in place—what are mere mortals that you should think about them, human beings that you should care for them? Yet you made them only a little lower than God and crowned them with glory and honor. You gave them charge of everything you made, putting all things under their authority" (Psalm 8:1-6 NLT).

God's Word says, "How precious are your thoughts about me, O God. They cannot be numbered! I can't even count them; they outnumber the grains of the sand! And when I wake up, you are still with me!" (Psalm 139:17, 18 NLT).

It is difficult for us to conceive that God thinks about you and me—that His thoughts toward us outnumber the grains of sand. The God who moves the wind, who brings the spring rain, who blankets the earth with freshly fallen snow and who named every star known and unknown to man also knows every breath you breathe. He knows every detail of your life. We never need to feel insignificant, small, rejected or less than anyone or anything because the God of the universe loves us with an everlasting love. (See Jeremiah 31:3.)

Pastor Craig Groeschel wrote in his book *Alter Ego*, "The way God made you was not by chance or accident. You are divinely inspired, with his divine intention to guide you. Once you begin to grasp who you are – and whose you are – you begin to understand why you're here and what to do."[1] You are not an accident!

A parable of two sons

Jesus communicated a parable referencing two sons, which is recorded in Matthew 21. A father was directing his sons to go work in the vineyard for the day. One son said he would not. The other said he would go and work, but did not go. The son who said he would not go ended up obeying and going to labor in the field. Jesus asked, "Which of the two obeyed his father?" (Matthew 21:31, NLT)

Jesus then takes time to explain the meaning of His parable. "I tell you the truth [speaking to the Pharisees], corrupt tax collectors and prostitutes will get into the Kingdom of God before you do. For John the Baptist came and showed you the right way to live, but you didn't believe him, while tax collectors and prostitutes did. And even when you saw this happening, you refused to believe him and repent of your sins" (Matthew 21:32, NLT).

Can you see the faces of the "religious" ones of Jesus' day just seething with anger over this? I can hear them muttering, "You mean to tell us these 'unclean' ones will enter the kingdom of God over us? How dare you!" But Jesus knew that those tax collectors and prostitutes had experienced a totally renewed heart.

Jesus invited everyone into His kingdom, without exception. He loves the criminal, the abuser, the addict, the unwed parent, the divorcee and the murderer. Without exception, God is after each and every one of us! No single credential, college degree or any amount of money impresses Jesus enough to let you into heaven. There is only one way to heaven, and it starts with a broken heart.

"You do not desire a sacrifice, or I would offer one. You do not want a burnt offering. The sacrifice you desire is a broken spirit. You will not reject a broken and repentant heart, O God" (Psalm 51:16, 17 NLT).

What has captured your heart?

What has captured your heart? What is your number one priority in life? The answer to that question will tell you what you value most. It will tell you where your heart is in relation to your search for personal identity. Please remember: in this search, your Creator has never given up on you, never rejected you and never said that you are beyond redemption. He created each of us with a purpose and destiny. He is longing for the "big reveal" in each of our lives. What potential does He see in you? Where does He desire to take you? Where has He called you? These questions all connect to the identity He has placed within you.

Another important step

To follow God's pathway, we must first know Him and know that He is good. We must trust Him and identify Him as our Lord and King. He desires that there be nothing between us, nothing to hold us back.

However, I have noticed one area that often prevents us from walking in the fullness of what God has for us. That area is woundedness from parents.

It is imperative to gain healing from these wounds because nothing affects the present like our past. While we addressed this somewhat earlier in the book, taking it a step deeper will allow us to fully enter the identity that our heavenly Father has for us. Here's why: we will most certainly struggle with God as our Father, a parent, if we still struggle with our earthly parents. If we have not forgiven those wounds from our past, they will block our relationships in the present and the future, especially with God as our heavenly Father. Throughout Scripture, family language is used: father, son, daughter and children. God created the family as the foundation for every culture on earth. But all too often, those family relationships provoke some of our deepest wounds.

Pain, a gift from God

Pain has a way of receiving our full attention. It is an indicator that something somewhere is wrong. Pain, at times, could actually be considered a gift.

As I stood over my wife in the emergency room, I felt helpless and teary. They were poking her, prodding, and sticking her with needles. She had been experiencing severe abdominal pain for two days and had finally agreed to go to the hospital. Now, a CAT scan was being scheduled. The doctors needed to discover what was wrong.

Physical pain tries to reveal something. Doctors pour over us attempting to diagnose the condition so they can come up with a treatment. Tests, blood work and vital signs are taken. We rush to find the cause of the pain in order to bring the cure.

Unfortunately, we often perceive emotional pain in a different way. We tell ourselves things like, "Time heals. The pain will go away...eventually." It doesn't. It remains undiagnosed. It settles deep into our soul and tries to hide itself. We cover it up with laughter and a "not going to let it bother me" kind of attitude. However, the pain becomes more severe and grows like a cancer, eating away at us. It can become infected and, at just the wrong time, surface in another form that is familiar or unfamiliar to us.

Mary's appendix had ruptured and poison filled her abdominal area. She needed emergency surgery that night and IV antibiotics for over twenty-four hours. When wounds from our past rupture, poison can enter our minds, our emotional realm and our spiritual realm. I have experienced that very thing in my life.

Blaming my father

I blamed my father for most everything negative in my life. After all, aren't parents supposed to be kind, generous and loving? Aren't they supposed to place their children first? Yes—and no. Not every parent is whole enough to be all those things to their children, as each one is in a different stage of healing and growing up themselves. But still, I expected perfection from my father. He was older, wiser and stronger than me. I apportioned all the blame for my messed-up life to him. For a while that worked.

Then one day I heard God whisper these words: "It is true, Steve, you did not have a perfect father, but you were never a perfect son and you, yourself, are not a perfect father." Talk about hitting the proverbial nail on the head with the hammer. God was confronting me, kindly, with His truth. I decided that day the blame game was over and that I would take Jesus' prescription to forgive as I had been forgiven. It was the only way forward. It would be the only way I would really find God as my heavenly Father and not project upon Him that imperfect image of my earthy father.

God's words to me were strikingly true. I was not a perfect father as much as I tried to be. I messed up with my children, perhaps in a different way than my father, but made plenty of mistakes nonetheless. And then God reminded me of something else.

God, our perfect Father

God is the perfect Father. He loves us perfectly. He forgives us perfectly. He disciplines us perfectly. He has our best interest in mind. God created a perfect garden within a perfect world. He created mankind and placed him there with the perfect job. He then created the perfect life mate for Adam. Yet by the time we reach Genesis chapter three, they were walking away from Him. Not long after that, in chapter four, Adam and Eve's son committed murder in a fit of rage.

Can you imagine? From a perfect world and a perfect relationship with God, the next generation committed murder.

I once heard of a leader who will not place anyone in leadership without asking the potential leader about their relationship with their earthly father. There is a lot of wisdom in that question. It relates to how we see ourselves. In our pre- and post-marital book, *Called Together*,[2] couples answer questions about their parents and their present relationships. We ask them to retrieve a word of blessing from their parents. We ask them to identify how they are similar to their parents and we ask them to write a letter of appreciation to their parents.

Is this line of questioning unreasonable or intrusive? For some, it might seem to be. But how they answer those questions gives us keen insight into how healed they are from past parent wounds, if there are any.

When in a dating relationship, observing and understanding how the person you are dating relates with his or her parents will make you more aware of these dynamics. Carryover from those relationships will enter the marriage, no matter how much we attempt to keep it out or cover it up. If there is a "No Trespassing" sign on this area of someone's life, beware.

Before we move on, perhaps this is a good time to stop and take an in-depth assessment of your relationship with your parents, even if they are no longer on this earth. Have you expressed forgiveness toward them? Have you asked them to forgive you for your wrongdoing? Have you forgiven yourself for those errors or failures that you walked in while growing up? Have you been able to release those lifelong hurts accumulated over many years? Because of your new identity in Christ, you no longer need to hold any parent, sibling or family member captive. Neither you nor they can pay the penalty for the transgression because that penalty has already been paid for by God's Son.

In the book *Transforming the Prodigal Soul,* author Scott Prickett writes, "Bad choices are driven by wounded souls. I helped this young woman connect the dots between the hurt arising from abandonment by her father and her use of drugs to mask the pain. We worked backwards...to the lie regarding her worth. In the wound of her father's abandonment, the lie that she was worthless and unlovable took root. It became her truth, her identity."[3]

Wounds lead to lies

Wounds will do that; they will produce lies. Those lies over time become our truths and attach themselves to our identity. That is why wounds from parents are so pervasive and can produce deeper hurts than those from most other relationships. Wounds from parents can become more severe because those relationships are so meaningful to each of us.

If you find yourself becoming hurt over and over, you are effectively creating a cycle of hurt and pain within yourself. We must, according to God's Word, "put off" this "earthly nature" from the ways we "used to walk," receiving hurt after hurt, and "put on" our "new self...the image of [our] Creator." (See Colossians 3:1-14.) "Bear with each other and forgive one another if any of you has a grievance against someone. Forgive as the Lord forgave you. And over all these virtues put on love, which binds them all together in perfect unity" (Colossians 3:13, 14).

Consider, once again, prayerfully walking through the seven steps to forgiveness in Appendix 1. Take a step of faith and speak an audible, verbal release to anyone that you have held onto for hurting or wounding you. While they may never know you have done this, you will feel a thorough cleansing from the inside out. There is no greater feeling than the feeling of total forgiveness and the release of the one you have held captive in your heart.

This one step, initiating forgiveness, can spare you years of torment and turmoil in your search for security and identity. Further, this one step can affect every other relationship you encounter in life. Dealing with parent wounds is essential in finding personal freedom.

Your bloodline has changed

You no longer belong to the bloodline of your biological family with all of its sin, dysfunction, illnesses, addictions, mental illness or history of wrong behavior. You now follow the bloodline of the family of Christ and the proof is in the Word of God. You are justified, redeemed, reconciled, free and purchased by His blood.

We have been justified by His blood. – Romans 5:9

We have redemption through His blood. – Ephesians 1:7

We are reconciled by His blood. – Colossians 1:20

We are freed from our sins by His blood. – Revelation 1:5

We have been purchased by His blood. – Revelation 5:9

Because of the cross, your family identity is now and forever found in the family of the Son of God.

"See how very much our Father loves us, for he calls us his children, and that is what we are! But the people who belong to this world don't recognize that we are God's children because they don't know him. Dear friends, we are already God's children, but he has not yet shown us what we will be like when Christ appears. But we do know that we will be like him, for we will see him as he really is. And all who have this eager expectation will keep themselves pure, just as he is pure" (I John 3:1-3).

Playing the blame game

I once heard someone say that constantly blaming others will keep us from growing. It is a sure way to not accept personal responsibility. Blame will cause us to shift our need to change over to others whom we desire to change. Simply stated, we cannot change anyone, only ourselves. I cannot change my parents. It is up to me how I determine to react to my history with my parents. Unless I take full responsibility, I will not experience change and personal growth.

One day I was thinking about the process I went through to be healed of family wounds, then took time to write them down. This is not a once-and-done process, but could require a second, a third and perhaps many revisited deliberations, because occasionally we regress in our healing. I cannot say for sure that you need to go through each of the steps below, but I would ask you to concentrate on those that God shows you as being presently applicable to your life.

Steps for healing family wounds
Recognize that my heavenly Father is not angry with me.
If God were mean-spirited or out to "get me," I'd already be "got." Instead, He placed all His anger at sin and disobedience on His Son on the cross.

Acknowledge that my heavenly Father planned me from eternity. He so much wanted me born that the family I was born into was and is inconsequential. He so much desired a relationship with me, that according to Acts 17:24-28, this is the time and the season I am appointed to be on earth that I would be loved by Him. Remember that when the gospel was presented to me, I asked for forgiveness of my sin and received the unconditional love of my Savior. I became a son or daughter of God.

Stop blaming earthly parents for all the issues in my life. They were not perfect. The revelation from God is, "You were never a perfect son or daughter." To this day, I am neither a perfect father or mother nor a perfect son or daughter. I had to stop blaming my earthly parent(s) and realize that each of them carries his or her own generational pain as well.

Receive more of God's love for myself. In doing so, I receive more of God's love for my earthly parents and family. I am a child of the King and a vital part of His kingdom. Through me He changes culture, even family culture. I am an adopted son who now cries, "Abba! Father!" (Romans 8:15)

Rest in the truth that I am no longer in need of the approval of my earthly father or mother, now that I know the approval of my heavenly Father. Romans 15:7 says, "Accept one another, then, just as Christ accepted you." I am accepted.

Hear God speaking the words that were spoken over Jesus, "This is my beloved son, in whom I am well pleased." Find identity and esteem not in who I think I should be, but in who I already am in Christ. I was destined for adoption as a son, according to His will and His purpose (Ephesians 1:5, 6).

Embrace the truth that life is not about me, my stuff, my need for healing or my brokenness. If it were solely about me, I would still be broken and be walking in the curses of the generations before me. Christ became a curse for me so that the curses from my father's father to my father to me and to my children are broken through His death on the cross. "Christ redeemed us from the curse of the law by becoming a curse for us" (Galatians 3:13).

Surrender any need for retribution or self-justification. I do not need to "get even" with anyone but instead pursue wholeness, maturity, security and sanctification. Jesus took my need for human justification by being the only Just One who can justify. (Romans 3:21-31). I am justified by faith.

Set healthy boundaries. I speak the truth in love with respect and a spirit of honor to my parents, my family and myself.

My father meets Someone

Regardless of who my father was, he was always loved and cherished by his heavenly Father. I had to come to believe that. My father could not pay the penalty for his own sin or the hurt that he caused. He needed the freedom that I found in Jesus. So I committed myself to pray for him and reach out to love him decade after decade. Did he deserve it? My answer to that has always been: did I deserve the love and forgiveness of God? No, but somehow God broke through and loved me anyway.

I did not love perfectly, but my heart was set on believing that my father could find the Christ that I had found way back in high school. And I believe he did. Here's how.

My mother had just suffered a severe heart attack and needed quadruple bypass surgery. She came through her surgery and rehabilitation quite well. In the meantime, my wife was caring for her father-in-law and the domestic needs of their home. One morning at the breakfast table she began speaking with him about his need for salvation and forgiveness of sin. She asked, "Dad, what if that heart attack had happened to you? Would you have been ready for eternity?" He replied, "I hope so." Mary said, "You can be sure, if you will ask Jesus into your life and ask Him to forgive you of your wrongdoing. Would you like to pray with me?"

It was the appointed time and the appointed place. My father loved his daughter-in-law like his own daughter, and he responded to her request. Before she could begin to pray, he began to communicate with God on his own. He ended his conversation with God by saying, "In the name of the Father, the Son and the Holy Ghost." It was a beautiful, sweet and sincere prayer and one that brings me joy to this day.

God is our identity mirror

Our identity is not based upon what we were or who we were. Author Dale Mast in his book *And David Perceived He Was King*, wrote, "[God] is our identity mirror. How we see Him is directly connected to how we see ourselves.... Your identity flows from your Father God to you, His son. What you have been saved from is not as great as what you have been saved for."[4] I like this radical shift in thinking because through the grace of God and the identity from God, we can treat people for who they are becoming rather than who they once were, as in the case of my father. Without this shift, relationships could be permanently marred by our unwillingness to be released from the wounds and lies found in our past.

We are being conformed

Each one of us is being conformed to the image of Jesus as we follow Him. We are growing into a transformation of identity day by day as we walk in obedience to His voice (Romans 12:1, 2). The Kendrick brothers write in their book *Defined: Who God Says You Are*, "Everything [Jesus] said and did flowed out of His identity. His teaching was not just brilliant instruction but was modeled by His life.... Jesus did not merely declare bold things, but He backed them up with actions and power. After proclaiming, 'I am the resurrection and the life,' for example, He immediately confirmed it by raising a dead man (Lazarus) from the grave. His life and ministry demonstrated that (1) knowing our God-given identity is a key priority for each of us, and (2) allowing God to be the One to help us discover it and live it out is foundational to fulfilling our purpose in life."[5]

Our identity must guide who we are becoming. With this new identity we have new authority, so that everything we say and do flows out of our identity in Christ. This is the goal of God in our lives and the goal of our life in God. This then is where it all ends, "But we know that when Christ appears, we shall be like him, for we shall see him as he is. All who have this hope in him purify themselves, just as he is pure" (I John 3:2, 3).

We shall be like Him. We shall walk in His identity, His life and His purpose. There is no greater life to be lived than the one in which we know who we are and Who we serve.

I invite you to read the prayer below, then consider praying for your own personal freedom. May your identity be forever found in the One who sacrificed His life for you.

Prayer of confession and identity

Dear Heavenly Father, out of my personal brokenness I have allowed things into my life, both known and unknown, that do not honor You. I confess to You my need for ongoing healing and restoration. I give You freedom to help me expose any areas of filth in my life. I give permission for You, the One who was broken for me, to reveal and bring to light rebellion, deception, independence, insecurity, comparison, compulsions, guardedness, self-justification, pride, critical judgment of myself and all other ungodly beliefs. I repent for any and all of these evils and trust You to do the work of healing that only You can do.

I now come to renounce the beliefs, the thoughts, the emotions and the reactions that the evil one has perpetrated in my life from these beliefs. This is not who I am in You. By Your grace I am a son/daughter, forgiven, regenerated, redeemed, restored and filled, as well as sealed with the Holy Spirit of God, no longer to be afflicted or harassed in these areas again.

My identity is fully and solely in who You say that I am. I am Yours and You are mine. I now know that I possess the mind of Christ and can think His thoughts. I am being renewed day by day and I know God's love is lavished upon me. I have been chosen by God and I can do all things through His Son who gives me the strength. God esteems me as His child and I am justified from all things broken in my past, present and future. I know now that I am qualified to share in the inheritance of Christ and I am loved with an everlasting love. This is my identity and my destiny!

In Jesus' name, Amen.

> *Once you had no identity as a people;*
> *now you are God's people.*
> I Peter 2:10 NLT

ENDNOTES

1. Craig Groeschel, *Alter Ego: Becoming Who God Says You Are* (Grand Rapids, MI: Zondervan, 2013).

2. Steve and Mary Prokopchak, *Called Together* (Shippensburg, PA: Destiny Image Publishers, 2013).

3. Scott Prickett, *Transforming the Prodigal Soul,* (Hurst, TX: Encounter. Encourage. Engage., 2017).

4. Dale Mast, *And David Perceived He Was King: Identity; The Key to Your Destiny* (Maitland, FL: Xulon Press, 2015).

5. Kendrick Brothers, *Defined: Who God Says You Are* (Nashville, TN: B&H Publishing Group, 2019).

My children shall be mighty
on the earth; wealth and
riches are in my house.

Psalm 112:2, 3

God will not take His love
away from my children.

Psalm 89:33

My children will stand firm in their faith.

Isaiah 7:9

My children will not turn
to the right or to the left;
they will walk in the way of the Lord,
that they may live and prosper.

Deuteronomy 5:32-34

PART 5: A CHILD'S SECURITY AND IDENTITY

CHAPTER SIXTEEN

The Heart of a Child

I am different. Not less. — Temple Grandin

Today you are you, that is truer than true. There is no one alive who is youer than you. — Dr. Seuss

I will be a Father to you, and you will be my sons and daughters. — I Corinthians 6:18

My favorite party invitation ever came from my friend's daughter who was about to celebrate her fifth birthday. I, along with her many little girlfriends, each received an invitation to her birthday "tea party." I responded with a hardy "yes." I would be there with a gift for her special day.

We sat around her table in her little chairs, drinking air from her little plastic cups of make-believe tea. My little blonde-haired friend smiled from ear to ear. She seemed so happy to be with a half a dozen squealing-with-delight little girls and one, much older, much taller, graying adult man.

I look back on that day with delight. That same little lady is studying at a local university now. She is an amazing young woman who knows who she is, whose she is and what her identity in her Savior is. How did she get there? I'll let her tell you.

In her own words

"Almost every morning at the bus stop my dad would call after us and say, 'You are blessed!' My mother would have devotions downstairs every morning, often reading a part of the Bible passage out loud as we played or did other tasks. If my siblings or I would say something negative or untruthful about ourselves or one another when we were growing up, my parents were always quick to replace the lie with a biblical truth, continually speaking life and love into our insecurities.

"There are scriptural truths that have been spoken over my life so many times that I will never forget them. They are buried so deeply within me that I know whatever happens in life I will forever fall back on those foundations.

"Now as a young adult, I often find myself relying on the truth of my identity in Christ. When things are difficult, I know that I am a child of God and there is nothing that I can do to change that. My parents set an example of what the Father's love looks like and gave me security in knowing there is nothing I could ever do to lose the Father's love or my parents' love."

Building a strong sense of identity in a child

Even as newborns, children recognize smells and the voices of those around them. While my children were still in their mother's womb, I would talk with them, pray over them, and let them know who I was and how we anticipated their birth. We would even read stories to them in utero. From the womb we wanted our children to know their worth and value. When born, each of my children recognized my voice.

Children also know and recognize strangers early on in life. They will typically not go into just anyone's arms if they do not recognize the smell or the voice. This new voice may feel strange to them and they may resist. Even tiny babies recognize differences as well as similarities.

It is said that children are not born with identities; those identities are formed over time from belonging, acceptance and affirmation, safe relationships with family, community (like extended family or church family) and their environment. Children receive messages concerning their identity that are spoken and unspoken. Most children recognize a response of shame, rejection or disapproval without one single word being verbalized.

A child's identity is further influenced by other contributing factors such as personal self-concept built by long-term relationships, memories of life events that help to build their life stories, being listened to, opportunities to explore, making decisions, experiencing failure and even observing how conflict is dealt with.

Relationships build identity

When children have positive, life-giving and loving relationships in their life, they will thrive. However, when children experience a negative, rejection-filled relationship, they will develop insecurities quite quickly. The most confident children have spent time with confident, supportive, accepting, caring and loving parents along with other persons. These persons have shown them loving approval, personal value and have let them know they are worthy of attention.

It is the relationships within a child's life that help to build a positive sense of identity. They are foundational to how they see themselves. Children tend to believe what they are told by the meaningful and important relationships in their life. For example, if I tell my daughter 3 + 3 = 6, she'll say, "Okay, Daddy, 3 + 3 = 6."

If her older brothers tell her the next day that the sum of 4 + 2 = 6, she will disagree because the day before she was told that 3 + 3 = 6 by her father, the voice that she recognizes as one of the most important in her life. Your pre-school children think in a one-dimensional manner. They do not think abstractly. They cannot decipher truth. They know and believe what you—the parent or the meaningful relationships in their life—tell them.

A child receives their identity through how they perceive the adults in their life perceiving them. When I tell my daughter that she's beautiful, she will believe that she is beautiful. You see, someone, namely her father, who is very important to her and who she trusts, told her something about herself. She has no reason to not believe it. Her thinking would go something like this: "If Daddy, whom I love and trust, tells me I'm beautiful, then I must be beautiful." She may not even know what "beautiful" is or means. However, she will go ahead and tell her brothers she is beautiful. They may not agree, but she will still believe it. Her brothers, while important to her, do not carry the weight that her father does in her life.

If I, as a parent, tell my children they are stupid, dumb, bad, worthless, or have no value, they will believe those things and act accordingly. Sometimes the negative words do not even need to be spoken, but how we say something to our child can also affect the child's interpretation of those messages with a negative result. Today we would call this emotional abuse. Years ago, it was simply punishment through shame or keeping children "in their rightful place."

The first stage of a child discovering his worth, value and identity is through the eyes of those who are important to him. The second is similar but has more to do with performance.

It is not long until we as parents expect things from our children. We expect them to do their chores, keep their rooms clean and finish their homework. When they do, we may reward them. When they don't, we are sure to let them know about it. Don't misunderstand me here. Expectations are not wrong; chores are not wrong; rewards are not wrong; words of correction are not wrong. What is wrong is if you develop within your child this formula: accomplishment + performance = approval/reward.

Performance versus approval

God has expectations of His children, but it is not our performances or our accomplishments that gain His approval. God is perfect, yet He is not into perfectionism. In our mere existence, He approves of us.

When you brought your newborn son or daughter home from the hospital, did you expect anything of him or her? Did you say, "Here's the refrigerator; when you're hungry, go ahead and grab a bite to eat"? In actuality, you expected to do everything for this child without return. It was lots of hard work and sleepless nights. In this baby's mere existence, you approved of him or her. You had no expectation of performance. That baby, without earning it, had your approval.

When your child begins to relate his or her performance to your approval, he begins to equate what he does as more important than who he is. Ask anyone who felt that he could not perform well enough to meet his parents' standard, and he'll tell you that he did not feel good about himself.

I've made my share of mistakes as a parent, but if you or I are relating identity or self-esteem to what our child accomplishes, we are wrong. God is not a harsh taskmaster who only gives His approval when we accomplish something for Him. Before Adam could accomplish anything for his Creator, the Word of God says, "God saw all that He had made, and it was very good" (Genesis 1:31). Adam was "very good."

The answer to a child's healthy identity is not a high esteem originating from some form of performance. The answer is a God-realized love and approval along with your love, acceptance and approval of your child. These two main ingredients are foundational to your child's healthy identity.

I must correct and reward my children. It is part of life. However, while reward and correction have to do with behavior, love and acceptance is related to one's personhood. In their mere existence, my children are important to me. I always approve of them as individuals. They can never do anything to not be my children or to cause me to stop loving them.

Strong and affirmative encouragement and approval from parents and grandparents will help your child to feel safe, capable, optimistic, well-adjusted and positive. In reality, most role models that are positive, encouraging and life-giving to a child will help to build a positive identity. We must take action to keep our children from negative, demeaning or destructive influences.

Proverbs 18:21 reveals, "The tongue can bring death or life" (NLT). Just as my young friend's father did in the story at the start of this chapter, speak words of life and affirmation to your children. In this way, you will help grow their security and identity.

A heartbreaking example

My son enjoyed school until second grade—when his teacher spent one whole year conversing negatively toward him, speaking words of critical judgment, chastising him unfairly and punishing him through constant scorn and shame.

As we discovered far too late, it seemed this teacher's mode of operation was to single out, with each new class, one student and turn him or her into her yearlong target of ridicule. It was a display of power and control at its worst.

Sadly, our son never told us how bad it was. He suffered from this treatment for the whole school year. We finally discovered what happened to him in two ways. First, the alarm was sounded by another classroom teacher who watched the behavior of this teacher and then called us in to the school to disclose what she observed. Second, we sat down with our son and told him we had learned about what had so unfairly and undeservedly happened to him through another teacher. We then asked him to rehearse everything he could remember from what he experienced with his second-grade teacher. He sat there in tears, sharing his experiences as we wrote three pages of handwritten responses on a large legal note pad.

It broke our hearts. We started an intentional campaign of telling him over and over he was not "bad," listening to his story and letting him know we would talk with the teacher and the principal of the school. It took years for his wounds to heal. That school year dramatically changed him in numerous ways. He was so deeply hurt, ostracized and humiliated in front of his classmates, but finally rescued in a sense by another teacher who showed him love and acceptance and, of course, by parents who went to battle for him.

Your children are bombarded by messages on a daily basis. We can't filter them all, but we can avert some of them. We might protect our children from negative, mean-spirited or abusive kids or inept adults. Yet one of the bigger negative influences is the media, including television, mandated public school courses and reading materials that do not uphold positive values.

Family values that help build healthy identity

When pornography is accessible within the public library system, on computers, through teachers who hold very different values than we do or by the media, children, with persistent exposure to these unhealthy influences, will experience strong negative effects upon their identity. Helping your children to be involved in activities they enjoy, activities which build positive life messages and organizations which build the spirit of a child will help to replace the negative media voices clamoring for their constant attention.

When you choose activities like camping, children and youth activities in your local church, sports clubs or other positive, life-building activities, you will promote something positive in your child.

Our family participated in several mission trips to serve others overseas. These trips built something extremely constructive in our children's identities as they learned to see the needs of others and to help meet those needs. It realistically taught them to not only focus on themselves, but to focus on the needs of others, especially some in less prosperous cultures.

We reached out to neighbors and the less fortunate. We involved them in many small groups that were family-oriented, fun and life-giving. We involved them in work which gave them an identity in accomplishing and completing a task. We engaged in regular family devotions, desiring to build truths that originated from God's Word and biblical values. We taught our children to love God because He first loved them. We introduced them to a relationship with Christ.

Josh McDowell once said, "Rules and regulations without relationship cause rebellion." If we make our faith about rules and regulations, we are not building identity; we are building a system of hierarchy toward achievement which could foster rebellion. We must model a living faith lest children begin to question our words as being meaningless. Then, when we set boundaries, we have reason beyond ourselves for the importance of those boundaries.

Teaching and modeling healthy, Bible-based values to your children will give them a foundation of belief that goes beyond yourself as parent, your child or their personal achievement. When we teach our children the things that Jesus taught us, for example, treating others as you desire to be treated, being a servant, blessing those who curse you, giving to those in need and loving even those who do not love you back, we instill the groundwork required for a healthy esteem and identity. When your family values giving your best, trying your hardest and doing things with all your might, you do not need to always be the winner in order to know who you are. When our children begin to understand they cannot achieve or aspire to their identity by their own self-effort, they will be miles ahead of their peers.

A child's identity and their sexuality

In the world we live in today, we are faced with a whole new category of child rearing and sexuality. When politicians are creating laws that concern changing gender assignments and when our schools are teaching curriculum that can be based on the present feelings of culture in our society, we as parents must know where we stand and how we will train our children through the truth of God's Word.

Much of the teaching today connecting gender identity with sexuality in primary school and high school curriculum would not be based on biblical truths or from God's definition of marriage and procreation. Unfortunately, these current thoughts, campaigns and misguided voices are not based on science but more so upon feelings. And, we are aware of the fact that feelings regularly change in the minds and hearts of children, pre-teens and teens.

When a teacher tells children in their classroom that they are neither boy or girl, and then to insist that using such gender terminology is sexist, children can become enormously confused. Further, if they are receiving one message at home and a very different message at school, they can become additionally confused.

My wife and I took the time to investigate our children's school's sex ed curriculum. We, at times, chose to opt our children out of certain classes because we did not agree with the perspective being taught. However, that material was mild compared to what parents must be alerted to today.

I encourage you to be an active parent, discuss curriculum with teachers and, if the values are different than you are desiring your children to be taught, be sure to work through that material together with your child or remove them from the class altogether.

Children are naturally inquisitive, and their sexual development will provoke more questions. These questions must be answered and not avoided by you, the parent. Meanwhile, understand they will be bombarded by messages from the media, their friends, their school, video games and even the cartoons they watch. Never turn a blind eye; be relentlessly and conscientiously aware of what messages your children are hearing throughout their development. It is our job to teach our children a healthy understanding of their sexuality.

Our children's sexual identity is a biological truth, and God's intention was specific. When we tell our children they are a "good boy" or an "awesome girl," we are affirming God's plan of two biological sexes. Further, a father and a mother are a picture of these facts. Remember, many research-ers believe that the greatest level of development in your child occurs before their school years begin. That means you can lay the foundation of God's creative acts from the book of Genesis, highlighting His truths about creating men and women to complement each other.

Showing children constant affection, acceptance, affirmation and unconditional, unquestionable love will help to grow happy, healthy and well-adjusted young men and women.

Girls becoming boys[1]

Why are so many girls now desiring to identify as a different sex? In an excellent Prager University video, Abigail Shrier, author of the book *Irreversible Damage: The Transgender Craze Seducing Our Daughters*, states that transgenderism has been studied for many years, but that it wasn't until more recent times that study involved more girls than boys. What has changed?

Shrier shares that in 2016 Brown University public health researcher Lisa Littman began to study this sudden spike in the trans identification of teenage girls. Her conclusions came to the fact that social media and peer influence had a lot to do with this change. That's because the message has become, "If you feel uncomfortable in your body, you are most likely trans."

There is hardly a teenager that doesn't at one time or another feel uncomfortable within their own body. By adding social media, comparison, depression, anxiety and confu-sion, the incidents of this uncomfortableness increase. In making the huge jump to offer testosterone or some form of surgery—more than likely adding further harm and for some irreversible, life-altering emotional and physical damage—

"professionals" are offering a "solution" that only leads to more confusion.

Many of these teens who have looked to social media and their peers for answers can now also view videos from teens who are saying it was a huge mistake to follow such a radical route as to alter their body and to take drugs to inhibit normal hormonal growth.

As parents, we must monitor and decrease our child's social media intake. We must protect our children from gender ideology teaching in our schools and we need to be present as adults and parents. Loving and listening to our children through the sexually confusing times found in the teenage years will in the end pay off as we speak a voice of reason and truth.

Our daughter understood

When our daughter began her university studies, she discovered something about her classmates as she also discovered something about herself. She observed the insecurity and the lack of identity among her peers and was troubled by their directionless lifestyles. She sent us this email.

Momma and Daddy,

While this was on my mind I thought I'd talk to you about it. I've been having a lot of good conversations with kids lately. I love these kids to death, but they are so insecure; it's sad. They have really low self-images, not many goals for their lives, feel as though they're not worth anyone's time and are hopeless that they will ever find the persons they are to spend the rest of their life with. I'm trying desperately to figure out what went wrong.... [They are] walking around like God is powerless to do anything to change their situation.

I just wanted to thank you guys that you did whatever it took to ensure that I was not an insecure person. You affirmed me in every way possible, encouraged my gifts, talents and preferences. You required excellence, but never demanded perfection. And you always made sure that I knew that home was a safe place where I was accepted for who I was regardless of what the outside world told me. Mentally, emotionally and most importantly, spiritually, I can recall few times that I have truly been insecure.

Thank you for instilling the security and identity in me to be able to believe that [God] can do all those things. I have the security to believe that no matter what happens in life, no matter what people think about me or tell me, that I am a beloved daughter of an Almighty King who has declared me holy, undeserving as I am. I love you guys and the more I see, the more I am grateful and the more I rejoice in my upbringing.

Now, as her parents, we would simply love to take all the credit for what she described, but we could not. We realize there is no guarantee in raising and training our children. We do our best to instill God's values and be a living example of His unconditional love, show acceptance and honor and pray, pray, pray.

Author Jim Anderson says it this way concerning our daughters and women in general, "[The] message today is that a woman's primary value is sexual. And, because her value is sexual, she better cultivate it and train herself to walk a certain way, talk a certain way, stand a certain way, look a certain way, and dress a certain way or she is going to be rejected, alone and forgotten. It is our job as fathers and leaders to fill the hearts of our daughters with the love and attention they need and to proclaim God's true identity over them, thereby protecting them from giving way to the assault of lies and deception that constantly bombards them."[2]

The same is true of sons. Our sons desperately need the affirmation and attention of their mother and father calling forth their true identity, masculinity and value.

We must teach our children that the external part of themselves is of value, but not nearly as much as the internal person, their heart, and their spirit. We use the external today to attract, but that attraction will never become a relationship that lasts a lifetime. We see television shows of children competing as models. There is hardly a worse life course to take our children on because it is sure to crash into comparison, disillusionment and deep disappointment.

When speaking to singles, we often tell them to not pursue marriage but rather to pursue maturity, because it's the mature persons who will be able to maintain a lasting relationship. As a young man or a young woman builds those inner qualities of character, security, selflessness, identity in Christ and direction, they will become mature and attractive.

When my son-in-law asked to marry my daughter, I gave him "the speech." I told him how much our daughter is loved and cherished by us, her parents. I told him how we value her and esteem her as a woman of God. I told him we would not desire anyone to ever hurt her or harm her in any way. She was our only daughter. To that he quickly said, "Yes, sir." And then I added, even more than being our daughter, she is God's daughter and God wants His daughter to be cherished, protected and loved in every way possible.

God values each person too much to allow anyone to be reckless with them, place them in harm's way, take advantage of them or devalue them in any conceivable way.

Another young person's story

This life story is from Josh, a friend of mine who found his identity in sports as a child and as a young man.

"Sports were a massive part of my life from a young age. My parents told me my first word was 'ball'! As soon as I was able, I joined organized sports, playing baseball from kindergarten through college. I loved competing, training, and playing, but underlying all of this was the misplaced identity that sports would forge in me through those formative years.

"There were so many positive outcomes of baseball in my life: work ethic, teamwork, physical fitness, true brotherhood, the pursuit of goals and many others. I would not trade those lessons for anything. However, what also occurred through my formative years in sports was a strong core belief and formula that **what I did defined my worth**. If I worked hard, I would receive playing time and if I received playing time, I would have the chance to succeed. If I succeeded, then the world would affirm me and I would know I had value.

"Everything came to a head my junior year of college. I was slated to be a strong leader on my baseball team. But things did not go as planned. For the first time, I came face to face with failure. My batting average plummeted lower than it had ever been despite the fact that I had the experience, skill set and ability to succeed. As the season slipped away, I was eventually benched.

"It was during this very trial the greatest breakthrough in my life occurred. Finally, I had the opportunity to recognize the foundation upon which I had been building my life—the affirmation of others. I was now beginning to see how every source of frustration, anxiety or depressive thought process stemmed from the fact that I had given the world around me the power to define my worth. It was during this season that I was forced to the Cross to receive the truth, grace, love and promises of God over my life. I made a conscious decision to stop building my life upon the broken equation that what I do defines my worth and began living with the truth that **what He did defines my worth**."

I love this story because it relates to so many of us who were also entrenched in different types of positive and negative identity attachments. If we continue to walk in those false identities throughout our adult years, we will inevitably pass them on to our children.

If you are building your family around yourself, sometimes unknowingly your insecurities and false identities will be passed on. But if you are building your family around Christ, you will build for eternity in the soul of your child.

Unconditional love

I was sitting at breakfast with a friend of mine complaining about how my sons seemed to be disrespectful toward me at times. I told him that I would not have dared to say some of the same things to my own father. He looked straight back at me and said, "That's because you feared your father. Your sons do not fear you and the reason they do not fear you is because they know your unconditional love." It was so true.

The Bible tells us that love casts out fear (I John 4:18). When we are feeling fear, we are not feeling love. When we are loving, we are not engaging in fear. Subsequently, when your children know your love, rest in your love, and experience your unconditional love, they will not be afraid. Their security and identity will grow exponentially. But even greater than this love is the unconditional love of God as their heavenly Father.

The secret to this process is not to build yourself in your child, but rather, build Christ. In Galatians 4:19, Paul the Apostle wrote, "My dear children, for whom I am again in the pains of childbirth until Christ is formed in you." Paul's goal was to form or to build Christ, not himself. I love the picture this presents because all the security and all the identity your child needs are found in Christ Jesus, not in you.

In the book *The Father You've Always Wanted*, author Ed McGlasson writes, "When our identity comes from God, we are set free from the limitations of performing for earthbound crowds. When we lay aside the desire to make a name for ourselves, we start to trust the Father to name us, which sets us free to spend our lives loving the Father we have always wanted."[3]

Do you desire to pass on God's blessings of security and identity to your children? If so, you as the parent must walk in the knowledge of those things. The more you know of God's provision to you in these areas, the more you will be able to instill these principles in your children's lives. The more security they see in you, the more security they will walk in.

We have a choice to walk in the brokenness of our past or to walk in freedom for today. If we come from a home that did not bless us or pass on these truths, then we need to learn how to bless our children or build Christ's life in them. Be sure of this: you will have a direct positive or negative effect upon your children for which you will be held accountable.

Concluding words on parenting

Being a parent is time-consuming, albeit one of the most rewarding, jobs on earth. When we desire our children to succeed, the reward becomes even greater. Parents who take the time to study their children and determine their specific needs, gifts and personalities will also find ways to help build security and identity through prayerfully building the life of Christ in each one.

Our children will help hold us accountable to who we are, who we trust and how we see ourselves. They will learn to identify our insecurities and push buttons in those same areas. Most children read adults better than adults realize. I am amazed at how my three-year-old grandson can understand my jokes. I am also amazed at how he knows exactly what to do to irritate his older brother or his grandmother.

Finally, parenting requires a huge level of humility. If we approach our parenting with a spirit of humility, we will be able to admit when we are wrong. We will also be able to apologize to our children, thus allowing God to use our children to change us. The older our children become, the quicker they will recognize our pride.

Please read Appendix 4, which explains ten more significant steps we can take to help build positive identity and self-esteem in our children. Each step will increase your effectiveness as a parent in these areas.

REFLECT AND DISCUSS

1. Share some of the differences between a loving and life-giving relationship and one that is negative and life-draining.

2. Can you share any ways in which your parents helped to build a healthy sense of security and identity within you?

3. In what ways can you identify with this negative formula: accomplishment + performance = approval or reward?

4. Can you share some family values that help to build a healthy identity?

5. How do your children know your unconditional love?

Note: For many more scriptures like those we began this chapter with, see a prayer tract I wrote entitled *Praying For My Children.*[4]

Another helpful resource

Irreversible Damage: The Transgender Craze Seducing Our Daughters by Abigail Shrier (Note: This is not a Christian book.)

ENDNOTES

1. This section adapted from Abigail Shrier, "Why Girls Become Boys," March 29, 2021, Prager University, video, 5:44, prageru.com/video/why-girls-become-boys.

2. Jim Anderson, *Unmasked: Exposing the Cultural Sexual Assault* (Franklin, TN: Carpenter's Son Publishing, 2012), 100.

3. Ed Tandy McGlasson, *The Father You've Always Wanted* (Ada, MI: Baker Books, 2013).

4. Steve Prokopchak, *Praying for My Children* (Lititz, PA: House to House Publications, 2007).

Because you are sons, God sent the Spirit of His Son into our hearts, the Spirit who calls out, Abba, Father.

Galatians 6:4

You are no longer a slave, to live in fear; the spirit you received brought about your adoption to sonship.

Romans 8:15

You were marked in Christ by a seal, the promised Holy Spirit.

Ephesians 1:13

He will keep you firm to the end, so that you will be blameless on the day of our Lord Jesus Christ.

I Corinthians 1:8

Final
Words

"There are two great days in a person's life—the day we are born and the day we discover why." — William Barclay

It has been the goal of this book for you to discover why you were born and to never let go of those truths.

In the Scriptures, God chose to call Himself "Abba" or "Daddy." It has always intrigued me that He used family language. Jesus repeatedly said that He only did what He saw His Father doing. If Jesus, the Son of God, looked to His Father, how much more do we need to get lost in His approval, esteem, identity and love? The following verses describe this relationship so accurately.

"The mature children of God are those who are moved by the impulses of the Holy Spirit. And you did not receive the 'spirit of religious duty,' leading you back into the fear of never being good enough. But you have received the 'Spirit of full acceptance,' enfolding you into the family of God. And you will never feel orphaned, for as he rises up within us, our spirits join him in saying the words of tender affection, 'Beloved Father!' For the Holy Spirit makes God's fatherhood real to us as he whispers into our innermost being, 'You are God's beloved child!'" (Romans 8:14-16, The Passion Translation)

No one will force you to receive your security and identity in the Father's love and acceptance, not even God Himself. According to the verses above, He says you are already good enough. He desires that you receive the "Spirit of acceptance" and approval. You are part of His family, never an orphan. Allow His Holy Spirit to make His Fatherhood real to you as He whispers in your innermost being: "You are God's beloved child!"

It is said that we become like those whom we spend time with. We will pick up their language, their mannerisms and sometimes their attitudes. Spending time with God is never wasted. As we learn His language, His Word, His mannerisms and His attitudes, we will find ourselves becoming more and more secure in that identity. You will no longer be who you once were or thought you should be. You will discover **the distinctiveness of you!**

What marvelous love the Father has extended to us!
Just look at it—we're called children of God!
That's who we really are.... That's exactly who we are....
And that's only the beginning. Who knows how we'll end
up! ... We'll see him—and in seeing him, become like him.
I John 3:1, 2 The Message

Seven Steps
of Forgiveness

1. Choose to forgive.

Forgiveness begins with a simple decision to obey God and forgive those who have hurt me. Jesus made it clear in Matthew 18:35 that this decision to forgive is to be from the heart. We are to forgive wholeheartedly, not holding back or keeping any resentment. Forgiveness starts not with feelings, but with a decision. Verbalize this decision by faith and confess aloud, "In Jesus' name, I choose to forgive _____."

2. Confess your sin to God.

Ephesians 4:32 reminds us we are to forgive one another, even as God through Christ forgave us. Even more, God desires for all people to know forgiveness. He sent His Son, Jesus, to die to make that possible. Withholding forgiveness can stop people from experiencing God's forgiveness. Yet God is always ready to forgive those who call on Him. (See Psalm 86:5.) Accept unforgiveness as sin and confess it to God. Then receive God's forgiveness, accepting it just as you would accept a gift from someone.

3. Ask forgiveness from those you wronged.

We are responsible to restore relationship with anyone who has anything against us. (See Matthew 5:23, 24.) Accept responsibility for the wrong you have done and ask for forgiveness. If you are unaware of what you did wrong, ask God to show you. If you do not have a genuine sorrow or repentance, stop first and prayerfully ask God to show you how you hurt that person and how they may have felt. Allow

God to give you a whole new understanding and sensitivity toward that person.

4. Ask God to bless the person who hurt you.

"Bless those who curse you, and pray for those who spitefully use you" (Luke 6:28 NKJV). Ask God to truly bless the person who hurt you. As you do this, follow the example of Jesus in asking God to bless him!

5. Do something nice for the person who hurt you.

"Do good to those who hate you" (Luke 6:27 NKJV). "Do not be overcome by evil, but overcome evil with good" (Romans 12:21 NKJV). This could be accomplished by complimenting that person or serving them in some way. Ask God; He will show you something that will be meaningful to that person.

6. Accept the person the way they are, even if they are wrong.

Do not defend what they do, but defend them. You do not necessarily need to approve of what they are doing, but treat them with dignity, respect, love and kindness anyway. "Therefore receive one another, just as Christ also received us, to the glory of God" (Romans 15:7 NKJV).

7. Look at this person through the eyes of faith.

Do not concentrate on areas of weakness, sin or irritation. Rather, concentrate on seeing this person as God designed them. Follow Abraham's example, and by faith see things that are not as they appear. (See Romans 4:16-21.) Begin to think and speak positively about this person. (See 1 Corinthians 13:4-7.) Love "believes all things and hopes all things."

Who I Am in Christ

Throughout this book, you have read scriptures about who you are in Christ. I trust they have brought you to a place of wholeness. Here they are again, along with others, to allow for continued meditation, study and personal heart change.

I am highly esteemed ....Daniel 9:23

I am now God's child .... 1 John 3:2

I am born of the imperishable seed of God's Word ..1 Peter 1:23

I am loved by Christ and freed from my sins .... Revelation 1:5

I am forgiven all my sins ....Ephesians 1:7

I am justified from all things .... Acts 13:39

I am the righteousness of God ....2 Corinthians 5:21

I am free from all condemnation .... Romans 8:1

I am free from my past ....Philippians 3:13

I am a new creature ....2 Corinthians 5:17

I am the temple of the Holy Spirit ....1 Corinthians 6:19

I am redeemed from the curse of the law .... Galatians 3:13

I am reconciled to God ....2 Corinthians 5:18

I am loved; God's Son sacrificed Himself for me .... 1 John 4:10

I am a saint and loved by God .... Romans 1:7

I am the head and not the tail ....Deuteronomy 28:13

I am called of God by the grace given in Christ ..... 2 Timothy 1:9

I have been given fullness in Christ ....Colossians 2:10

I am rescued from the power of darkness .... Colossians 1:13

I am accepted by Christ .... Romans 15:7

I am the salt of the earth ....Matthew 5:13

I am the light of the world ....Matthew 5:14

I am dead to sin .... Romans 6:2

I am alive to God .... Romans 6:11

I am seated with Christ in heavenly realms .... Ephesians 2:6

I am a king and a priest to God .... Revelation 1:6

I am loved with an everlasting love .... Jeremiah 31:3

I am an heir of God, a joint heir with Christ .... Romans 8:17

I am qualified to share in the inheritance
   of the kingdom of light .... Colossians 1:12

I am more than a conqueror .... Romans 8:37

I am healed by the wounds of Jesus ....1 Peter 2:24

I was known by God before
   I was formed in the womb .... Jeremiah 1:5; Ephesians 1:4

I am in Christ Jesus by God's act .... 1 Corinthians 1:30

I am kept by God's power ....1 Peter 1:5

I am sealed with the promised Holy Spirit .... Ephesians 1:13

I am not condemned; I have everlasting life .... John 5:24

I am being conformed to the image of God's Son ... Romans 8:29

I am crucified with Christ, nevertheless I live .... Galatians 2:20

I have been given all things that pertain to life ....2 Peter 1:3

I have been blessed with every spiritual blessing .. Ephesians 1:3

I am a partaker of the divine nature ....2 Peter 1:4

I have peace with God .... Romans 5:1

I am a chosen royal priest ....1 Peter 2:9

I can do all things through Christ .... Philippians 4:13

I have all my needs met by God according
   to His riches in glory in Christ Jesus .... Philippians 4:19

I am kept strong and blameless to the end ....1 Corinthians 1:8

I am chosen by Him .... 1 Thessalonians 1:4

I am born of God and I overcome the world .... 1 John 5:4

I have a guaranteed inheritance .... Ephesians 1:14

I am a fellow citizen in God's household .... Ephesians 2:19

Christ's truth has set me free .... John 8:32

I am in Jesus Christ's hands .... John 10:28

I am holy, without blemish
and free from accusation .... Colossians 1:22
I have eyes to see God's eternal purpose .... 2 Corinthians 4:18
Christ is being formed in me .... Galatians 4:19
I am anointed by the Holy One .... 1 John 2:20
God's love is lavished upon me .... 1 John 3:1
I am kept from falling and presented without fault .... Jude 24
I am God's house .... Hebrews 3:6
God has given me a spirit of power, of love
and of self-discipline .... 2 Timothy 1:7
I am convinced that He is able to guard
what I have entrusted to Him .... 2 Timothy 1:12
He has considered me faithful and
appointed me to His service .... 1 Timothy 1:12
I am justified by faith .... Romans 3:28
The Spirit Himself intercedes for me .... Romans 8:26
Inwardly I am being renewed day by day .... 2 Corinthians 4:16
For freedom Christ has set me free .... Galatians 5:1
I am held together by Him .... Colossians 1:17
I have the mind of Christ .... 1 Corinthians 2:16
I am called to build Christ in others .... Colossians 1:28
I am a son and an heir of God.................................. Galatians 4:7
I am protected by the power of Jesus' name.............. John 17:11

How Should the Church Respond to Sexual Identity?

Mother Teresa is quoted as saying, "Love one person at a time." The key, the attractant to a group of people called the church, is love.

Before I became a follower of Jesus, I was invited to a rather Pentecostal church. I had never stepped foot inside such a place. The level of praise, excitement and shouting took me way out of my comfort zone toward nervousness and a desire to run. I had no idea what would happen next. It was all new to me.

As I look back at that experience, I no longer remember the oddness of the moment or the persons who grabbed me and shook my hand vigorously or the people dressed in jeans and others in three-piece suits. But what I do remember, what profoundly sticks in my memory is the love I felt. Hug after hug, all given in love. Everything took a back seat to what I was feeling deeply and had not felt in a church setting ever before.

No one judged me for not singing. No one judged me for not raising my hands and no one judged me for not saying, "Praise the Lord!" They just loved. It attracted me to the One they loved.

That is the power of love. Love draws out the beauty of another. Love accepts without judgment or condemnation. Jesus loved and paid close attention to anyone who sincerely sought Him. He loved His neighbor as Himself.

This is where the church starts and ends—love. We love because He first loved. It is also where we mess up because sometimes we get judgement in front of love, and no one is attracted to judgment. It's not a condemning voice that draws anyone to repentance. Jeremiah wrote, "With loving kindness I have drawn you" (Jeremiah 31:3). Romans tells us that, "God's kindness leads you toward repentance" (Romans 2:4).

When you or I claim to follow Christ, then love must be our means to a confused soul. If they do not know our love, they will not receive our message.

A welcoming community

The local church must welcome the broken. If any community in any culture could offer a safe place, it should be the church. It is our job to care for, receive, counsel and love the broken. These persons need a family, a spiritual family who accepts them for who they are and where they are, with great faith for where they can someday be.

We all need a place to belong. We all need genuine friends—a place to connect. In loving those who are broken down by life's burdens, we do not have to be professional counselors. We do need to share with them the love of the Counselor.

For years I worked with a man who was diagnosed as "paranoid schizophrenic and depressed." Very few persons knew how to relate to him and even fewer wanted to. But the Spirit of God gave me a deep compassion for this "unlovely" man. He knew who accepted him and he knew who ridiculed or belittled him. He knew who to talk to and he knew who was "safe." Everyone, even this very disturbed man, is worthy of the love of God and, therefore, worthy of our love.

The book of I John says something that relates: "Whoever claims to love God yet hates a brother or sister is a liar. For whoever does not love their brother and sister, whom they have seen, cannot love God, whom they have not seen. And he has given us this command: Anyone who loves God must also love their brother and sister" (I John 4:20, 21).

One evening our local news revealed that a man in my wife's home church shot and killed his wife, his daughter and then himself. I laid in bed that night telling my wife that a man who commits double homicide and then suicide has just entered hell. He was an elder in his church and a well-known believer in Christ. I will never forget the words I heard in my spirit just as I made that statement. "How do you know where he is? How do you know his state of mind? And how do you know his heart?" I was stunned. The obvious answer was that I did not know.

Regardless of the struggle in people's lives, we do not know their hearts. I have counseled plenty of persons who lived with life-controlling sins and at the same time claimed Jesus to be their personal Savior. God knows their heart.

The senior pastor of a Foursquare church in Los Angeles, CA, Nancy Eskijian, said concerning those who attend her church, "So how do we approach gay people inside or outside the church – or transsexual or transgendered people, for that matter? We demonstrate God's love in practical ways and with genuine interest, just as Christ did. We approach them with compassion, healing, and truth in the doses they can receive, just as Christ did. We move toward them as we are led by the Holy Spirit, just as Christ did."[1]

No compromise with God's Word

At the same time, we do not compromise the Word of God. If someone is living life in error and not obeying the Word, we fully love them but do not place them in leadership in the local church. We dare not compromise the Scriptures for the sake of acceptance. We are not ashamed of the gospel, because it is the power of God for salvation for all. (Romans 1:16)

I will be forever thankful for leaders in my life who confronted my sin scripturally and in a healthy way. I will forever be thankful that my heavenly Father is a Father who disciplines and will not compromise His Word. In the book of James, we have a promise that connects to exactly what we are talking about. James reminds us to confess our sin to one another and to pray for one another. James promises that prayer, the prayer of a righteous person, is powerful. He then writes, "My brothers and sisters, if one of you should wander from the truth and someone should bring that person back, remember this: Whoever turns a sinner from the error of their way will save them from death and cover over a multitude of sins" (James 5:19-20).

What an amazing promise. When we walk in humility and take a mature position, longing for the one in error to leave their error, we can, "save them from death and cover over a multitude of sin." That is the church in prayerful, loving action.

Love must be sincere. Hate what is evil; cling to what is good. Be devoted to one another in love. Honor one another above yourselves.... Share with the Lord's people who are in need. Practice hospitality.... Rejoice with those who rejoice; mourn with those who mourn.... Do not be proud, but be willing to associate with people of low position. Do not be conceited (Romans 12:9, 10, 13, 16).

ENDNOTE

1. Nancy Eskijian, "The Truth about Our Gay Dilemma," *Charisma*, February 2013, https://www.charismamag.com/life/culture/16574-the-truth-about-our-gay-dilemma.

Ten Areas to Build Healthy Identity in Children

1. Employ corrections, not punishment.

One of the most difficult things to do as a parent is to reinforce a boundary and provide appropriate discipline. All too often, children have this uncanny ability to bring the worst out of us as parents. Sometimes we might overcorrect them or dish out punishment because we are angry. This should be avoided.

Punishment has to do with me preserving my right to be angry and maintaining my posture as the one in charge. It says that my child must pay for what he or she did wrong. Punishment is often done out of anger and lacks any training toward change. Put simply, it is the more powerful parent enforcing his or her will upon the weaker child. Punishment is about inflicting shame and pain for wrongdoing.

Correction, on the other hand, is not just about reward and punishment; it is more about challenging actions and shaping the will in a life-giving manner. In this way, the spirit of the child is guided and formed. It considers what is best for the child.

Correction takes time to administer because it includes instruction toward a different and healthier future. Punishment on the other hand is normally abrupt, reactionary and often given with little thought. Proverbs 29:15 says that the rod of *correction* imparts life. Job 5:17 reminds us that God also provides correction: "Blessed is the man whom God corrects; so do not despise the discipline of the Almighty."

Correction provides training with love. It takes into consideration the gifts deposited within each child. Punishment provides pain, but no lasting effort toward change.

2. Train your children in the way they should go.

The book of Proverbs tells us to train our children in the way *they* should go. This can be interpreted as each child's bent, calling and gifts. Draw those gifts out. Find ways to encourage them and make use of them in order for your child to grow in his or her own identity. (See Proverbs 22:6.)

When our son was three years old, he would remove the pots and pans from the kitchen cabinet, place them on the floor upside down, sit on one, grab two wooden spoons and then play the "drums." It didn't take much to realize that we could identify his gifts and to do everything within our power to help him follow his interests.

Our son eventually progressed in his craft to the extent that he was drumming on two albums produced in Nashville. It truly was a calling for him.

3. Empower your children, rather than being powerful over them.

Far too many parents train their children to view Mom and Dad as having all power and control over them. Even when we do not try to give this impression, it somehow comes across fairly often. For example, have you ever heard a parent say, "Because I said so"? And then there is this one: "You will do this (fill in the blank) or you will not be able to do this (fill in the blank)."

These statements may work in the first several years of life, but as children mature, the commandeering approach needs to be adjusted. If it is not, we will train our child into thinking that they just need to resign themselves to our power. The use of power is often void of relationship. A void of relationship creates a void of security.

One day, in the life of every child, that power will be resisted, tested or simply ignored. Powerless children become victims because powerless people view themselves as victims. Powerless people do not have to take responsibility for their actions; they can blame others. Eventually, powerless people may want everything provided for them. But there is an alternative. Empower your children to think and reason and make choices of their own. While providing proper boundaries, teach them to make decisions rather than you as the parent deciding everything for them.

For example, if your child is playing with their food rather than eating during a meal, try this: ask your child (as is age appropriate), "Would you like to finish your meal and then play a little longer with your friend outside or not finish your meal and stay inside to play by yourself?"

To a teenager you might say, "If you wash the car, you can use it tonight to see your friends, but if you choose not to wash the car, you'll have to find a ride on your own. It's your choice." Choices empower our children.

What's the difference? By giving a choice, you are empowering your child to reason, think through the process and choose their own conclusion and consequences (again, as is age appropriate). Powerful children will do powerful things one day as they take responsibility for their decisions.

As we train our children, some areas are negotiable and some are not. This is similar to the scenario in which some classes in high school are required and some are electives. I might say to my child that dress is a negotiable, but modesty in dress is nonnegotiable. It is primarily in the negotiable areas where we can give our children freedom of choice, helping to empower as they approach those all-important stages of interdependence and finally independence.

4. Keep communication sacred.

Have a meal together every day and talk as a family. Discuss the good, the bad and the challenges. As parents, share about your workday and start the discussion. If we are not open as parents, neither will our children be open about their daily experiences. Have conversations about anything and everything at all age levels. Give each one your attention as they share and require that no one be laughed at but rather laughed with.

Ask questions instead of making statements. Questions require a response from your children while statements do not. Questions offer opportunity for them to expound on certain subjects and can lead to really important details. Looking for responses, opinions and input from your children emphasizes their value.

5. Teach your children the art of play without electronics.

Our son's pediatrician expressed to us as new parents, "Keep your child off the electronic games as long as you can. Teach him to play creatively, send him outside and go explore with him."

Did you know there is a National Toy Hall of Fame in Rochester, New York? Every year a new member is inducted into this toy hall of fame. In 2005, the cardboard box was inducted. What kid doesn't love to play in a cardboard box? One of my favorites was the toy that was inducted in 2008—a plain old stick. The stick was picked because of its "all-purpose, no-cost, recreational qualities." It is portable and versatile and "fosters learning creativity through play and imagination." It's the perfect price; it's all-natural; it's organic; there are no rules or complicated instructions for use. It can be a horse, a sword, a hockey stick, a fishing rod or a snowman's arms.

6. Train your children in the world of finances.

Teach your children about money, saving, spending, credit, debt and giving. Children who are trained in the proper use of money will have the financial skills that will be essential in the "real" world. We train them to understand and respect money, not to love money. We train them in financial stewardship from God's perspective.

Use the financial lessons you have learned as a teaching tool to those little ones in your life, either as a parent, a grandparent, or a caretaker. Their future teachers and employers will love you for it. Author and financial teacher Larry Burkett once said that we are not responsible for our children's decisions, but we are responsible for their training. Here are some important areas to train them in.

God owns it all. We are to be the best stewards of everything He shares with us.

Because God is so generous, teach generosity. There is no greater blessing than to teach your children the value of giving.

Teach the difference between self-discipline, delayed gratification and immediate self-gratification along with the direct consequences of each.

Give your children regular and meaningful responsibilities: jobs without pay such as picking up their toys. Do not give an unearned, free-ride allowance, but rather give your children regular jobs like mowing the lawn or folding the clothes that they can be paid for.

Teach your children to tithe and honor God's kingdom from every dollar earned or given to them. It is all God's, but discipline in regular giving grows a habit.

Teach your children to save a percentage of their income for the future (30-50%), even while designating a percentage that can be spent immediately.

Teach the difference between an asset and a liability (a consumable). Help them to understand the concept of investing and how that will help them beyond today into the future.

Develop a budget with your child as soon as they can comprehend the idea. Start a savings account (starting with a piggy bank) and when age appropriate, obtain a checking account and an ATM card. Teach them how to responsibly use and balance these accounts.

Train them in the proper use of credit and that the borrower is servant to the lender. Teach them the difference in borrowing for an asset versus a liability. Share with them the difference between paying interest and growing interest on their money and investments.

Share with your children your financial mistakes in a way that allows them to learn and benefit from them.

As appropriate, explain other financial concepts such as loans, taxes, utilities, owning a home, maintenance, buying a car, auto repairs, insurance, etc. Take the time to teach your children what God takes the time to teach you about money and His resources.

Financially savvy young persons are miles ahead of financially insecure persons. Learning financial responsibility will sow into one's identity to build further confidence and help keep them from certain financial failures.

7. **Do not talk down to your children or speak words of critical judgment.**

A recent study of primary school children centered on trying to discover the number one inhibitor to children's creativity and eventually to their performance. I was intrigued to know what these social scientists identified. While there were many ingredients, the area that stood out as the number one killer of creativity was *critical judgment*. Critical judgments are critical words that tear at one's spirit without mercy or grace. They involve criticizing something that is not necessarily changeable (e.g., a lack of athletic ability or academic ability). When words of critical judgment are cast upon another human being, that person begins to suffer a creativity crisis that can lead to an identity crisis.

When a child hears consistent words, tone of voice and nonverbal looks that say, "We never planned you; you were not wanted," they will begin to believe these words. Even when a child hears the words, "What's the matter with you?" or "Don't be so stupid," it indicates in a critical way there is something wrong with them. Their life will be scarred. Their demeanor, the look on their face, and their life expectations will take on this spirit of critical judgment. Proverbs tells us, "Reckless words pierce like a sword, but the tongue of the wise brings healing" (Proverbs 12:18).

8. **Teach your children how to resolve conflict.**

Having children to raise, to train and to love is a privilege that can be stretching, maturing, tiring and, quite often, exasperating. I loved being a parent and now love grandparenting. If you are serious about parenting, you realize at times it is more than you think you can handle. At those times, I wondered if I was raising my children or if my children were raising me.

An inability to resolve conflict will keep us stunted for life. Of the dozens and dozens of couples that have sat before me for marital counseling, few of them had any clue of how to actually resolve a conflict. They were experts at having them, but clueless at finding solutions. When you teach your children the skill of resolving conflict in a healthy way, you will impart a talent that will serve them for a lifetime in every relationship, every job and practically every life situation.

You and your spouse cannot have out-of-control arguments without resolve and expect to teach your children how to resolve life issues. You must push toward a healthy solution to the problem with compromise, thereby modeling healthy conflict resolution. When children can learn to resolve conflict, there will be more peace and joy in their life. They will experience less anxiety and far less sadness over broken relationships.

9. Speak words of blessing.

Reading through the Old Testament books of Genesis and Exodus lately has been a great reminder concerning the blessing of God to Abraham, Isaac and Jacob and the blessing of fathers to their children. It caused me to think about the fact that "the blessing" might be missing, dormant or decreasing among us as parents today.

When God speaks a blessing, He does not revoke it. Because of Joseph, the Egyptians were blessed. Even Potiphar, Joseph's boss, realized blessing from the exemplary life of Joseph. The Scripture says, "The blessing of the Lord was on everything Potiphar had, both in the house and in the field" (Genesis 39:5).

In the book of Exodus, a blessing was pronounced on food and water. Freedom from sickness was promised for those who blessed the Lord in worship. After all the plagues, when Pharaoh finally summoned Moses and Aaron in order to relent and allow the Israelites to leave Egypt, he said, "Take your flocks and herds, as you have said, and go. *And also bless me*" (Exodus 12:32).

10. Do not make your children your idol.

Your marriage was before children and will need to be a priority after your children are raised. My encouragement is to place God first, then your marriage and then your children. Our children, while extremely important, cannot be treated as idols. We are not called to worship them or their needs. Parents are not able to meet all the needs of their children, but we know Someone who can and will.

Further, we as parents are not to live our lives vicariously through our children. Parents who endeavor to do this are attempting to find their identity through their children. An example is to dress our young children in the latest, most expensive style of clothing. The children are unaware, but the adults around them notice and make comments of admiration concerning stylish dress.

Another area is sports. For example, you may not have excelled at sports, but your child does. You then live vicariously through your child's sports exploits and accomplishments. Yes, you are proud of your child, but you're more proud of the inferences and accolades you might receive because of your gifted child. You may be unknowingly entering into a competition for the admiration your child deserves.

Do not idolize your child or maintain the goal of becoming your child's best friend. You are not their peer; you are the adult. Choose to be the parent in each and every situation.

While these ten areas are not exhaustive, they encompass a lot of our day-to-day parenting. Do not let them overwhelm you; instead, read back over the above ten areas and pick one area to concentrate on. Perhaps take the time to write down three goals with that one area and begin to work on positive changes in your parenting. In the future, keep reviewing these ten areas. Choose another to work on, and then write down three new goals.

Other books by Steve Prokopchak

Called Together
Pre- and Postmarital Workbook

This unique workbook, designed for couple-to-couple mentoring use, prepares couples for a successful and God-honoring marriage. Down-to-earth biblical wisdom to help couples get off to a positive start. Includes post-marital checkups at three and nine months. Has sections for remarriage, intercultural marriages and remarriages of senior adults. By Steve and Mary Prokopchak, 250 pages: $19.99

Staying Together
Marriage: A Lifelong Affair

Read as a couple and together, you'll hear from what we've learned over more than 40 years of marriage, as well as from other couples whose marriages have endured heartbreak, hardship, and even infidelity. Whether you've been married for months, years or decades, now is the time to make sure you're in a marriage that's not just surviving, but thriving. By Steve and Mary Prokopchak, 251 pages: $16.99

The Biblical Role of Elders for Today's Church

Healthy leadership teams produce healthy churches! Follows New Testament principles for equipping church leadership teams: what the qualifications and responsibilities are, how elders should be chosen, how elders function as spiritual fathers and mothers, how elders should make decisions, resolve conflicts, and more. By Larry Kreider, Ron Myer, Steve Prokopchak, and Brian Sauder, 274 pages: $12.99

Who I Am in Christ Tract

Truth from God's Word to set you free. Dozens of scriptures describe who you are in Christ. Read them over and over, allowing the truth of God's Word to set you free. $1 with quantity discounts.

Praying for My Spouse/Children Tracts

Handy tools to help you pray! Includes dozens of scriptures to help you pray for your spouse or children. Pray them daily and see God work in his or her life! $1 and quantity discounts.

www.store.dcfi.org
call 800.848.5892
Check out the many discounts!

People Helping People series

With illustrations and discussion questions, these booklets are helpful for personal, small group and one-on-one mentoring.

Be Angry and Sin Not

Do you make excuses for your anger or for the anger of another? Or, have you been affected by an angry person? This booklet will give you biblical insight into how to make changes or help someone else. 36 pages: $4.99

Recognizing Emotional Dependency

This guide identifies and deals with emotionally dependent relationships. It gives examples from people's lives. Solutions and assignments help to further reveal how a person may be free of dependent relationships. 32 pages: $4.99

Thinking Right in a World that Thinks Wrong

If you desire to cling to your past, this booklet is not for you. If you want to change and move on in your Christian walk, then carefully work through this booklet as it analyzes and gives applicable scriptures with helpful illustrations about this process of change. 36 pages: $4.99

Counseling Basics
Helping You Help Others

Is counseling for the professional only? What do you do when a member of your small group or someone at work asks for advice? Where do you begin? 2 Corinthians 3:5-6 tells us, "Not that we are competent in ourselves to claim anything for ourselves, but our competence comes from God. He has made us competent as ministers." Learn to be an effective people helper. 112 pages: $14.99

In Pursuit of Obedience
Deepening Our Love for God through Obedience

Have you ever felt overwhelmed by the tremendous self-discipline outlined in scripture? God's love for us must be the foundation upon which we build our emotional, physical and spiritual health. Learn how God sets "love boundaries" for our lives. Ideal for small group study with its discussion questions and activities. 224 pages: $8.99

www.store.dcfi.org   call 800.848.5892
Check out the many discounts!

About Steve Prokopchak

Steve Prokopchak has been a marriage and family counselor for many years. Steve earned his master of human services degree from Lincoln University. As a member of the DOVE International and USA Apostolic Councils, Steve helps to provide oversight and direction for DOVE churches in the United States and the Caribbean. Steve's vision and heart's cry is to see people made whole in their personal lives, marriages and families. He travels regularly, ministering in churches across the nation and internationally, giving people the various leadership and counseling tools they need.

Steve and his wife, Mary, wrote *Called Together*, a unique workbook specifically designed for couple-to-couple pre- and postmarital mentoring use and *Staying Together*, a book helping married couples to build a strong and lasting relationship. Steve also authored a series of booklets called *People Helping People*, topics suitable for small groups. He co-authored the book *The Biblical Role of Elders for Today's Church* and is the author of *Counseling Basics* and *In Pursuit of Obedience*. Steve has had articles published in *Charisma* magazine, *Ministries Today* and *Cell Group Journal*.

Steve and Mary have been married for 46 years and have three married children. The Prokopchaks enjoy three grand-children and live in Elizabethtown, Pennsylvania.

Read Steve's weekly blog calledtogether.wordpress.com.